BUSINESS
HIS
WAY

IBUKUN AWOSIKA

Copyright © 2009 by Ibukun Awosika

BUSINESS HIS WAY
by Ibukun Awosika

Printed in the United States of America

ISBN 978-1-60791-506-5

All rights reserved solely by the author. The author guarantees all contents are original and do not infringe upon the legal rights of any other person or work. No part of this book may be reproduced, stored in a retrieval system, or transmitted, in any form or by any means, electronic, mechanical, photocopying, recording or otherwise, without the prior written permission of the author. The views expressed in this book are not necessarily those of the publisher.

Unless otherwise indicated, Bible quotations are taken from The Holy Bible. Copyright © 1982 by Thomas Nelson, Inc.

www.xulonpress.com

ACKNOWLEDGMENTS

Business His Way, as a public ministry, was born solely through the conviction, never ending push and encouragement of Pastors Taiwo and Bimbo Odukoya for us as a church to reach the business world with the message of God as it pertains to business.

I most definitely would never have taken the step to start the TV ministry nor write this book, except that you believed in me enough to push me into a destiny assignment. THANK YOU. Simple words, but definitely from the depths of my heart.

Many thanks to my Personal Assistant, Babatunde Oladele, for all the time spent on research for the book and the TV ministry.

To the main men in my life, ABIODUN,

OLUDOLA, OLAFUSIKA, and OLAMIPOSI, thank you for your love, encouragement and for allowing me to invade the privacy of your home by using it as my recording studio.

You guys mean more than the world to me. I love you more than words can express.

FOREWORD

When in 1992 the Lord led us to start the Business Fellowship at *The Fountain of Life Church* to be headed by Mrs Ibukun Awosika, little did we know it would turn out to be a ministry that would affect many in the church world and even beyond.

Seeing Mrs Awosika evolve over the years has pointed to the fact that building a successful business is obviously not an easy task. If it were, everybody who has ever started a business would have a successful venture today. In spite of the vast knowledge and resources available in our time, you will discover that many start very well only to get truncated midstream or plateau out early in business.

What that points to is the fact that

becoming a good business person is not automatic it takes time, efforts, skills and, in most cases, living conscious of God who is the author of increase (1 Corinthians 3:6).

The truth is, every business ought to be taken seriously; it must be approached like any other profession. Those who obtain lifelong success in it are those who are ready to pay the necessary price in education, training, hard work, character and everything it takes to stand out in a profession.

Amazingly, most of those who do not succeed in business are often those who are looking for an easy way out. In other words, they are not really called to business and so do not have passion for it. Such may seem to succeed temporarily but ultimately go the same way of gamblers who think that success is by chance.

In *Business His Way*, Ibukun Awosika provides a fresh look at time-tested biblical principles that have aided the emergence and sustenance of successful businesses, most of which have outlived their original owners. She teaches how to know whether or not you are called to business and considers the qualities of a business person. She also analyses the role of

FOREWORD

fear, honesty and partnership in business, and proffers solutions to the menacing issues of business bondage as well as bribery and corruption.

As a business person or a potential business person, I believe you are not looking for a get-rich-quick scheme; you are motivated by the desire to serve humanity and leave an inheritance for your children. That is why this book is for you. I assure you the information in it will set you on a journey to lifelong success, not only in your business, but also in your personal life.

Be blessed as you read.

Pastor Taiwo Odukoya,
Senior Pastor,
The Fountain of Life Church,
Ilupeju, Lagos.
Nigeria.

DEDICATION

To the many sons and daughters of God who are daily being told that it is impossible to succeed in the market place of today without compromises; but who have chosen - against all odds - to honour our God by conducting their businesses based on His word and the values He represents.

May your individual lights continue to shine as you allow the Master to shine through you.

I truly salute your courage.

TABLE OF CONTENT

Acknowledgments	III
Foreword	V
Dedication	IX
Introduction	13
1. Are You Called To Business?	19
2. Essential Qualities Of A Business Person	25
3. The Fear Factor In Business	41
4. Partnership	59
5. Honesty In Business	71
6. Business Bondage	79
7. Bribery & Corruption	101
8. Business FAQs	125

INTRODUCTION

The idea of **BUSINESS - HIS WAY** series was instituted in pursuance of our vision at The Fountain of Life Church *'to build the home and thus build the nation'* as well as *'to equip the saints for life and ministry.'*

Business His Way, in other words, means business transactions done in line with the way and standards that God has earmarked for business interactions in His word, the Holy Bible.

The question most people will probably ask is 'What has God got to do with business?' To answer that, we need to first ask ourselves this critical question, 'What has God got to do with life?'

Considering the fact that everything we are and do is His idea, this will help us to understand that He is also interested in the way we interact with one another at all levels of social interaction.

In the olden days, people did not rely much on written agreements and contracts to do business transactions. A word of honour was a word of honour. There was a lot of respect for what the other person said or promised to do in those days, and life went ahead like that.

In addition, most of the business schools in existence then were founded on biblical principles. They were more like Bible Schools raising businessmen, because their curricular were focused more on instilling integrity and building sound character in the people who were in business.

Unfortunately, this is not the case in this present time. Business, as it is done today, requires a lot of documentation, signing, and witnessing; with lawyers working back and forth in order to effect what was ordinarily done by mere word of mouth in the past. That is why it is fast becoming imperative that we resort to our Source and find out exactly what He has to say about business practices.

Business His Way was started as an avenue

INTRODUCTION

to share with those in the business community how God prescribed that business transactions be done, with the hope that a great country like ours would have a change of identity from that of a corrupt nation - as it is perceived in the international community - to one with a great people, of great character, from communities with great values.

You might have wondered why some businesses survive through many generations while others went under as soon as their owners were dead. It is because the ones that survive were built on and run by sound principles. Any business that is built on bad practices will disappear some day.

Let me share with you a statement credited to J.C Penny, the founder of the **J.C Penny Stores,** an acclaimed great businessman in his time. This man recognized that God and the Bible have a place in business, and despite the fact that he died years back in 1971, his business still remains till date. Hear what J.C Penny has to say:

"I think it is a good thing for...a businessman...to know something about the Bible. I was past thirty before I discovered that the Bible was a pretty fine

> *business textbook! I do not mean to be irreverent when I say that Jesus and Moses were two of the greatest salesmen the world had ever known. Just take one of the Bible's stated principles - and there are scores of others which might be picked out and see how it applies to business. I refer to the declaration that "if a man would be first amongst you, let him become your servant". That principle is at the foundation of business success. I think it would be a good idea if the business colleges would include the Bible in their list of textbooks. I suppose its value lies in the fact that it teaches character, which is the very foundation of success."*
>
> -J.C Penny (1875-1971)

That was a man who had taken the time to try it out and who had found that integrity and character are the core foundations for building a successful business that will live beyond the owner.

If all you do is to build a monument that cannot stand the test of time, what have you

INTRODUCTION

achieved? That is the reason the Bible cautions us not to be envious of the wicked; because even the ground on which they stood will not remember they ever walked on it when they are gone.

1

ARE YOU CALLED TO BUSINESS?

People go into business for different reasons. And many people are frustrated with their businesses for various reasons as well. But the primary question I will like to ask you is this; are you called to the business-line where you are presently operating? Or are you in the business because of any of the following reasons:
- Because you think it's a good idea to have a business of your own
- Because your friend or neighbour has been successful in business
- Because the uncle you admire most is a businessman

- Because you think it's easier to make money in business
- Because you want to be your own boss

Whilst there is nothing wrong with any of the above reasons, it is obvious that neither of them can be enough reason to build a sustainable and successful business. While it might be a good idea for you to have a business of your own, it is not necessarily the best idea for you as a person if that's not the place of your calling. You might even make a success of it, but you might never be fully satisfied and find contentment in it.

Your friend or your neighbour might be successful in a particular business, but who says that is the business where you would succeed? Even if you were called to business, the question is which particular business?

The uncle you admire the most is a businessman, but do you really know what kind of business he is doing? Or are you willing to do the things he is doing in order to succeed?

Many people say it is easier to make money in business. You need to talk with businessmen and women who are at the edge of packing up in order to know that indeed there are untold stories of losses and frustrations in business.

When you are called to business, you will find that you have a natural inclination for the business line you have chosen to pursue. You might ask; how do you identify what you are called to do? The truth is that God has given every man gifts and talents that are necessary for what He has called him to do.

Your first duty is to identify those gifts. They can be found in the things you are passionate about, in tasks and activities that you enjoy doing most, something you have a natural flair for, those things you are willing to die doing; things you are willing to do all of the time, there lie the business you are called to do.

Now someone might say, 'the things I like doing are not things one can do as a business.' That is not true! Every talent you possess has a business side to it, and it can be commercialised or converted into a profitable venture. Converting those talents into business is therefore dependent upon your seeking God, asking for His direction, seeking counsel from those who are already in that line, trying your hands out at it, and seeing what opportunities exist therein for enterprise.

Of course, you are expected to do some foundational works before starting off, one of which is finding out where needs exist in the area you perceived you are called to; where are people seeking for things that you can probably develop solutions for; or what is it that you see people do, but every time you see them do it, you think you can do it better.

The Bible says 'there is safety in the multitude of counsel' (Proverbs 11:14). When you have such ideas, or you see such opportunities, talk to one or two people who are already operating in that area, seek their counsel, add those counsels together, seek the face of God. Then move on it.

One of the reasons most people never launch out to do what they are called to do is because they are afraid of failure. If you perceive an opportunity in something, even if you try it and it fails, you would have learnt one way not to do it. But if it is something you are convinced you are called to do, the best thing you should do is to try other ways of doing it until you find the mix that works.

For every business opportunity you identify, there is a probability that one or two other people might have identified it too. However, only the man who is committed enough will invest the time and energy required to go the extra mile in order to proffer the solution that will make the difference, and therefore convert it into a profitable business.

5 WRONG REASONS TO GO INTO BUSINESS

Before bringing this discourse to an end, let me highlight some additional wrong reasons for anyone to go into business.
- Because you are sick and tired of being told what to do
- Because you want more freedom
- Because you feel unappreciated or undervalued in your present job
- Because you want to make a lot of money
- Because you want to improve your standard of living

These are all wrong reasons for you to want to start a business of your own. Even if you own your own business, your customers will tell you what to do, remember the saying "he who pays the piper dictates the tune"? It is a big fallacy to imagine that as a businessperson you will have great freedom of time. On the contrary, your work hours are no longer 9-5 from Monday to Friday, but rather anytime is a good time on any day of the week.

No matter how unappreciated or undervalued you are made to feel in your present job, what guarantee do you have that your employees and your customers, in your own business, will not make you feel the same way.

But if you are pursuing the call of God upon your life, and you are walking according to His plan and purpose, you will find joy in doing what He has called you to do. For then He will show you the way to go, give you understanding, and lead you to find fulfilment.

By pursuing character and integrity in business, you would discover that you could actually gain all. You can have a happy life, a good standard of living, make money, and yet you do not lose your soul or your family name in the process.

2

ESSENTIAL QUALITIES OF A BUSINESS PERSON

In the introductory chapter, we examined some tips that can help you to identify if you are called to business, and what kind of business you are called to. We also looked at some wrong reasons for anyone to go into business.

In this second chapter, we shall look at some qualities you need to possess in order to be successful as a businessperson:

1. Personal Development
The Bible says that 'a man's gift will make a way for

him and bring him before great men' (Proverbs 18:16). Whatever line of business God has called you to, the gift He has deposited in you will help you to pursue it. But it is also necessary that you seek to develop other qualities that are required to make your business venture a success.

It is one thing to have the raw desire and passion for what you want to do. But apart from your talents and natural abilities, there are other skills necessary for building a business. For instance, you need managerial skills and some knowledge of accounting to run a business successfully. This is because at the beginning of your business you will find yourself doing almost all the operational tasks. And the more you are equipped with some of the skills required to carry out these tasks, the better you are able to do them, and the better the services you provide for your clients.

2.   Focus

To build a successful business, you need to be focused. The day you make a decision about the particular line of business you want to do, you cannot afford to deviate from it and start to pursue

ESSENTIAL QUALITIES OF A BUSINESS PERSON

another one which seems more attractive at the moment; that will only make you a jack-of-all-trades and master of none.

At the starting point, there is a need for you to concentrate on giving all that you have to that business to nurture it. That is when people will see and appreciate your ability. It is not the time to say because selling GSM phones is the popular thing these days, then that is what you will do, whereas you have identified that photography is what you are called to do. If you do that, you will only end up splitting your resources, your time, and your concentration. And at the end of the day you will not be able to establish anything.

There is a point you get to in business where - having established one and having run it successfully - it will be easy for you to move on to another one. And people will be willing to help you; banks will be willing to support you, because you already have a good track record. The place that you start from is the opportunity you have to set up that track record.

3. High Sense Of Commitment

To show commitment, you will stay with what you

started. Commitment means that you give all your resources to what you do. And when you have challenges, you are not quick to run away.

At one forum I asked for people who have done different businesses over time. Quite a lot of people got up. Then I asked a particular young man among them how many years he had been in business. He said ten years. I further asked the number of businesses he had done in the ten years, and he answered seven or eight.

Do you know what that means? It means that if you divide his ten years in business by the eight businesses he had done, he had only given a year and some months to each business before he gave up on it and moved to the next one!

There is no business you will do that will not have its share of challenges, but if you have identified right from the outset that God has called you to it, and you know that God cannot lie, then when challenges come, you will stay with it until you find a solution.

For the person that has done eight businesses in ten years, imagine if he had invested those ten years into the one business that God has called him to do. In the first place, he would have been known

ESSENTIAL QUALITIES OF A BUSINESS PERSON

for the business, because he would have gained a respectable list of clientele - people that would have grown with him in the business in the course of time.

Secondly, he would have acquired a lot of skills that only come with time. He would have learnt certain skills that come in the course of operating a business. And there are costs-saving methods he would have learnt that only the process of time can avail one. Commitment to what you have chosen to do is important. The reason many people tend to change business is because someone they know has become prosperous in a particular line, and they also want to join the bandwagon.

But you have to find out first what God has really called you to do. What are the things that only you can do better than everyone else around? You are supposed to pursue those areas of natural advantage and stay committed to them. Commitment means that you nurture your enterprise until you succeed, and that you stay with it until you bring it to the breakthrough stage. It is important that you have commitment if you want to succeed.

4. A Devoted Spirit

You must also be devoted. Having a devoted spirit means that you are not just doing all you do physically, but you are also nurturing it spiritually. It means you are always praying for your business. Because if you say that God is the source of what you have chosen to do, you must also believe that He has the answer to every question that might arise in the course of your running the business.

When you encounter a challenge that seems beyond you, what you will simply do is go to your Source. You get on your knees and ask God for help; you ask Him to show you things you do not know; that He reveals to you solutions that nobody else around has thought of. And you can be assured that He would respond (Psalm 61:1-2).

Remember the story of Daniel in the Bible, when nobody else could give an interpretation to the dream of Nebuchadnezzar, Daniel went on his knees and asked God to reveal it to him. Only God has the secret to what no man knows. And because you are His child, He would give you everything you need to do what He has committed to you at every stage of the way. As you seek Him, He would be there to show you the way to go.

ESSENTIAL QUALITIES OF A BUSINESS PERSON

5. Staying Power

You must have a lot of staying power to be successful in business. That means you do not give up easily. Once you know the business God has called you to, the fact that there seems to be no great commercial gain there should not bother you, the Bible says God will make a way where there seems to be no way. When it seems that every door is shut, there is always a window somewhere that men do not see, but which God will reveal to you to move out of the ruts. But if you are quick to give up, that's the end. Because someone else with a greater staying power will stay a little longer, discover that hidden entry, and become the star in that business.

I have been in the same business for almost 20 years now, and I become quite amused whenever I come across some of my old friends and they ask me, "Are you still in that same business?"

I would then ask myself 'what else am I suppose to do?' 'Am I supposed to have changed business many times along the way?'

When you stay long in a business, you can only get better at it; because time has a value that nothing else can give to you. So you need to stick to what you have chosen to do. When you stay with it, you will eventually get to the top. That does not mean that you cannot venture into new areas or make new investments, but don't kill one business for another, except you are sure there is no way in it.

6.   Open-mindedness
This means that you are flexible and not rigid. The world is changing everyday. Things are changing so fast that you can't afford to be rigid, which is why the Bible says we should seek knowledge and understanding (Proverbs 4:7).

You must always be open-minded; you must be open to new ideas. You must listen to people around you. There is wisdom in every man. The person who cleans your office could be the one who has the solution to your problem. In other words, you must learn to place value on people; especially those around you. They are your blessing; they are the ones God has chosen to bless you with.

As a person, you have both personal assets and liabilities, and for every liability you have, the people around you are supposed to have the assets that will make up for it. It takes asset plus asset to succeed that is, your asset and that of others.

If you do not value people and treat them as

you want to be treated, they will not add value to you. But if you treat people as you want them to treat you, then you will have no problem going far in life and in business. You will have faithful and loyal people who will stand by you through every stage of your business. There will always be people that will cause you pain. Consider them as part of your "No pain, no gain" assets. There are things you can only learn from them. Don't waste your pain.

7. **Willingness To Seek Counsel**

Talking about counsel, the Bible says that 'in the multitude of counsellors, there is safety' (Proverbs 11:14).

To be successful in business, you must not be a know-it-all person. The general saying is that 'two heads are better than one'. And if you consider the Bible passage that says 'one shall put a thousand to flight, and two shall put ten thousand to flight' (Deut 32:30); you will realize that, in unity, there's always a chance to do more.

Counsel affords you diverse views on a matter. The truth is many people who do business or pursue a particular venture are so passionate about what they want to do that they become unreasonable in some things. They are so driven to accomplish their objectives that they overlook little details that could spell doom for their venture.

By taking counsel from other people, you are able to see external views. And if you are the kind of person who is open and responsive to counsel, especially from your wife, your parents, or people who have passed through the path you are about to follow, you will rarely miss the way.

In this regard, I would like to particularly address married men who aspire to go into a new business venture, but consider their wives as irrelevant to their pursuits. Most entrepreneurs tend to think that because they are the one who have the original business idea, then the other person won't have much to offer. This is far from the truth. Sometimes all you need to avoid stumbling in your pursuit is a novice's view of what you want to do. And if you are married, your spouse is supposed to enhance you in everything - your business inclusive. It is unfortunate though that the tendency to despise the partner's input is so common amongst us. But even more so in men.

The Bible describes the woman as a helpmate

for the man. That means there is something in your wife that will enhance your general performance in life, especially in your business or career. You should therefore cultivate the habit of seeking her input, just as you do from everyone else.

8. Ability To Make Good Decisions

Having sought counsel and relevant facts from different quarters on what you want to do, you need to know how to take the right decision.

Taking the right decision is a tall order. This is because many people are swayed by public opinion in their decision-making. But at the end of the day, you are solely responsible for the decision you take. The only litmus test you need in this area is to weigh whatever decision you are about to take against the Word of God. If such decision aligns with the tenets of the Holy Bible, then it is not likely you are wrong. If you read Psalm 1:1-3, it says:

Blessed is the man that walketh not in the counsel of the ungodly, nor standeth in the way of sinners, nor sitteth in the seat of the scornful. But his delight is in the law of the LORD; and in his law doth he meditate day and night. And he shall be like a tree planted by the rivers of water, that bringeth forth his fruit in his season; his leaf also shall not wither; and whatsoever he doeth shall prosper.

I want us to analyse this passage from the perspective of a businessman. The following are the characteristics of a businessperson that is referred to here:

THE *PSALM 1* BUSINESSPERSON
1. He does not run his business by ungodly principles: every decision he makes is related to the Word of God. What does the Word of God say? It does not permit that you steal, cheat, or do to others what you do not want them do to you. This command alone - not to do to others what you do not want them do to you - is enough guide to run a business successfully.

2. He does not follow the examples of sinners in his transactions: the common excuse one hears this day is that 'This is the way everybody does it.' Are you everybody? You are in the world, but not of the world. You are the example the world needs as the light of the world. For light to conform to darkness, it has to die.

ESSENTIAL QUALITIES OF A BUSINESS PERSON

With particular reference to Christians, a lot of us are Christians on Sunday mornings and a different kind of person the following morning. We have chosen to believe that it is impossible to do business by Christian standards. We have become schizophrenias, we are good on Sunday mornings, but once we get to the business place on Monday we become like the rest of the world. And we defend our lack of integrity with the excuse that the only way one can do business successfully in Nigeria is by compromises.

That is an absolute lie! There are a good number of individuals, even in this country, who are upright in all their business dealings. The Bible says we are 'the light of the world and the salt of the earth; we are the city that is standing on the hill' for the whole world to see. It takes one man to change a nation. It takes you choosing to do things the way the Bible commands, and not the way the world is doing it, to make a difference in your own ecosystem.

You can actually choose not to do business the way everyone else does, because a **Psalm 1 Businessperson** does not follow the example of sinners, no matter how profitable it may be. To the sinner, it is alright to sell goods to customers with false measures as if it is a full one. But when you read certain portions of the Bible, you will realize how such people are bringing curses upon themselves by their dishonest practices. For the Bible says, 'God despises uneven measure' (Proverbs 11:1).

3. He does not keep the company or enter into partnership with the scornful: this refers to those who blatantly walk contrary to the word of God. A **Psalm 1 Businessperson** does not align with people who scorn the wisdom and instructions of the word of God in their business process.

4. He delights in knowing and applying the laws of God to his every day life - his business inclusive: If you are a **Psalm 1 Businessman**, you will not be a Christian on Sunday and a non-Christian in your business on Monday. What you hear and say that a Christian should do is what you yourself will practice in your workplace.

You will not cheat your customers or mistreat your staff, because you are aware that they too are sons of God, and He equally cares about them. You will not hold back the wages of those who work for you because the Bible says that when they cry out to God He would hear them.

And God cannot be bribed; He is a just God. He will deal with every man according to his deeds, both seen and unseen. It is not a function of your status or your power. It is a function of His word. So, whoever you are, if you cheat a beggar on the street, you will account for it, because God deals with all men in fairness and sincerity.

The man who wants to succeed in business is the man that is conscious of the principles God has laid down in His word. And while seeking counsel and making decisions, he places value on things that are godly above all else. The decisions you take today will affect the things you do tomorrow.

Do you know what is going to happen tomorrow? The only person who knows both today and tomorrow is God. And if you include Him in your decision-making, you will avail yourself the advantage of both today and tomorrow. For God will lead you to make decisions today that He already knows the resultant effect tomorrow.

Most times we operate by what we see. But

our knowledge is limited because there is so much of tomorrow we do not know. We can guesstimate as much as we want, but there's only one person who controls the future. That is God. And every time we walk with Him and allow Him to influence our decision making process, we are sure we would succeed, because He will guide us in the way we should go as the Bible promises. And we are not likely to fail.

3

THE FEAR FACTOR IN BUSINESS

In this chapter, we shall examine **The Fear Factor in Business**. I am quite sure some of you must be wondering whatever that could mean. If you think deeply enough, you will realise that many people indeed have the ability to do some things better, but they make no attempt at all to do them because of their fear of what might be or happen if they do.

What is fear?
The overriding cause of fear in most of us is our

excessive obsession with ourselves: our limitations, our weaknesses, our inabilities and our inadequacies. In other words, fear is caused by our conclusion that - for whatever reason - we might not be able to do one thing or another.

KINDS OF FEAR
Different kinds of fear plague humanity, some of them are:

Fear of Failure
Many people have never taken the step required to start their dreamed business; take their business to the next level; or even take a definite decision to commit to one thing or the other because they are afraid of what will happen. They are paralysed by the fear that they might fail in the venture, and so they end up doing nothing. Some people even do not get married because they are afraid their marriage may not be successful.

Fear of Mistakes
This is another form of fear. Some people never take a step or attempt anything because they don't want to make mistakes. Now, life is full of mistakes.

Some of the mistakes we make are actually necessary for us to arrive at our destination. But if you are afraid of making mistakes, you will never discover, you will never find pleasant surprises, you will never walk into the unusual or exceptional.

And sometimes the abnormalities and rarities of life are what bring about or lead us to miracles and unusual findings. And the unusual findings are what make you a superstar, because what everybody else can easily find or have access to does not command much respect. The unusual things that you walk into are what separate you from the rest. Sometimes, a step that is considered a mistake may be the step to discovery. There is so much of the world to discover, why would you allow fear to stop you?

Fear of Rejection
Some have never loved, cared, committed themselves, nor show others what they are capable of just because they are afraid of being rejected. If you give something to somebody and he rejects it, it is that person's loss and not yours. Why should that bother you? Until you give it, you do not know if the

other person will accept it or not. But fear of rejection can stop you from ever loving, ever caring, ever committing, or even doing some of the things that make life worthwhile in itself.

Fear of Change

For instance, if you are used to doing some things in a certain way in business, and now that we are in a computer age everyone is saying another way is faster, more efficient, and more productive. But you say No, because you don't want to take any risk with all these new technologies and their challenges, and so decide to stick to what you know. That means you are afraid of change.

Sometimes, that which you know and stick to may render you redundant and irrelevant in the marketplace. And at the end of the day the business collapses or dies simply because you have refused to change.

Many factories have folded up because they stuck to using machines that have become obsolete as new technologies took over. And the manufacturers who produced the old machines are not even producing the items that they will need to work anymore. The time they needed to make the change, they did not do it then and at the end of the day, the business dies because they refused to adapt to change.

Yes, there will always be some element of fear, but that is the beauty of life. What does fear represent in business? The unknown. If we knew everything, life will be so boring and there will be no need to trust God for anything. There will be no need to believe that God is in control of our lives. We will have it all worked out. We won't even need God at all. But being able to trust God and take the step of faith is a function of resisting fear. There will be no need for faith if we allow fear to come in.

Change is a part of life. At one point or the other in life we have to make a change in our business or it will be forced on us. For instance, my line of business was greatly affected in 2004 when the Nigerian government announced a change of policy that resulted in a ban on the importation of furniture, which is my core area of business. Change became inevitable. I either go completely out of business or make a change in my business strategy, in line with the changing policy in the country.

I therefore had no choice but to comply with

the change in policy in order to continue my line of business or join the bandwagon of those that ended up becoming smugglers with the excuse that all they knew how to do was to import. And since the government has placed a ban on importation they just have to find a way to continue doing what they know how to do best. Would you rather not change than become a smuggler? I would rather change in line with the changes that are going on in the country than remain where I am and become a criminal by so doing. A criminal by the laws of the land, and a sinner by the laws of God.

Change is inevitable in life. One day you were born as a baby, and then you started to change and became a child. And from there you changed to become an adult, and from adulthood, you changed to become an old person. And one day you will change from life itself to death. That is a reality of life, change is real. We cannot afford to be afraid of change.

Fear of Confrontation
There are people that work in a place and have never voiced out exactly how they feel about the situation around them because they are afraid of

confrontation. They are either not pleased with their colleagues who boss it over them everyday, or with the way someone else talks to them. But they have never had the courage to say, "I don't like the way you talk to me. I don't mind if you advise me on one thing or the other. But talk to me in a decent manner and treat me with respect."

Sometimes you need to do that. But if you are afraid of confrontation, you will accept things you shouldn't have from people and they will assume that you are fine with it.

Sometimes as a business leader, your fear of confrontation prevents you from telling those that work for you that you don't like what they are doing. And what happens? They assume they are doing fine and keep on at it until the day you are not able to bear it anymore. By then it might have been too late to remedy the situation. And most times people who are afraid of confrontation are only able to communicate how they feel when they really lose their temper or their emotions get the better of them, which is not usually the best circumstance.

Fear of Success
This is interesting. You might ask, 'why would

anyone be afraid to succeed?' But interestingly enough, there are people who are afraid of what would happen if they succeed: how would they cope with the attention, how would they behave in the light of their new status?

A man might say, "I know that I'm competent and qualified to become the next General Manager of my company. But I also know that the last GM always had to go to cocktails and dinners with expatriates from foreign companies. How am I going to cope? I don't know how to handle the cutleries, speak flawless English, or how to mix with certain kinds of crowd."

What do you care? If you are confident in yourself, people will accept you as you are. The good news is that you can always equip yourself with the relevant knowledge on those things you don't know how to do but which you need to know in order to operate at the level that success has positioned you. And by so doing, you will be able to deal with the fear.

Sometimes the best way to deal with fear is to step right in and do the thing you fear. And most times when you do just that, you will discover that there isn't much to what you are afraid of. It is the thought process that builds fear in us rather than the real action itself.

Discovery is the biggest answer to everything you are afraid of. When you discover the real nature of that thing you are afraid of, you will realise that it is not as intimidating as you think it is. But you have to muster the boldness and confidence to do something, and ask God to help you. The Bible says that 'God did not give us the spirit of fear, but of love, power, and sound mind' (2 Timothy 1:7). With these we can overcome any situation that stands before us as an intimidating factor.

Fear is one of the barriers to people succeeding in life. Fear is not alone; it has many relatives such as worry, anxiety, self-doubts, and low self-esteem. And all of these combined are big enough to paralyse one's mind and make it difficult for you to make the necessary move to succeed.

Consider this reality of life; no matter how foolish or humorous someone else's fear may sound in your hearing, your own fear is always very real to you. In other words, someone may say "I'm afraid of heights." And if you are someone who delights in climbing mountains without giving it much thought, you will think the man who is afraid of heights is stupid because that is not a problem to you; whereas for him it is a matter of life and death. Fear can be so real if we allow it to take a foothold in our lives.

Let me share the stories of some historical figures who had experienced different forms of fear in their lifetime:

1. *Julius Caesar, a powerful military general and Roman emperor, was said to have a great fear for thunder.*

Can you count the number of times you have sat unperturbed in your house while it was thundering outside as it was about to rain? But imagine a man as great as Julius Caesar having an inordinate fear of thunder. That shows you how powerful fear can be if you allow it to take root in your life.

2. *Peter the Great, the Czar of Russia, and an imposing figure at six feet five inches tall, was said to be afraid of bridges. He crossed them only when there was no other alternative, route to take. And when he did, he trembled and cried like a child.*

Think about that. Imagine how many times you

have crossed bridges without any ado. To you it is as if you are walking on solid ground. But for a man who was a great ruler to fear crossing a bridge sounds quite ridiculous. That is how real fear can be if you allow it to germinate in your mind.

3. *Dr. Samuel Johnson, a British writer and literary critic, had a phobia about entering a room with any foot other than his left foot. Anytime he accidentally entered a room with the left foot, he backed out and entered again with his right foot. He took wanting to put his best foot forward to a ridiculous extreme!*

Talk about superstition. Remember that this man was neither a Nigerian nor an African. He was an educated, polished, and respected British scholar. But this is what can happen when you do not face your fear and overcome it.

How many times have you taken for granted the fact that you entered a room with a left or right foot? What do you care? Even when we were young and we were told that if you knock your right foot against something it is a sign of bad luck and vice versa. I cannot imagine how many times I have knocked my right foot against something and have thereafter walked into a miracle. It is simply a matter of your mindset and your ability to brace up to face your fear.

Any situation for which you can find a correlating reference in the Bible, you already have the solution to it. And since the Bible says 'God has not given us the spirit of fear, but of love, power and a sound mind' (2 Timothy 1:7), that means every time you face something that is manifesting as fear in your life, you should just hold on to the word of God and say "God has not given me the spirit of fear. I'm not afraid of this thing (say whatever it is)".

Then you should prayerfully square up to confront the situation. And you will discover that you can overcome most fears that try to overwhelm you.

THE EFFECTS OF FEAR

What are the effects of fear? Fear often breeds inaction. If you are afraid of failing, you will never act to succeed. If you are afraid of making mistakes, you will never do anything. You will never even discover that you can do something successfully without making a mistake.

THE FEAR FACTOR IN BUSINESS

Even if you make a mistake; so what? Who cares? Who says that you have to get it right the first time? When you do something once and miss it, you would have learned one way not to do it, and then you go on and do it differently the next time. If you learned 999 ways not to do something and finally get it right at the 1000th time, you can be sure there are not enough people who have the self-control, perseverance, and the will to do anything 1000 times before getting it right. That means you will be separated from the crowd because most people would have probably given up at the 10th or the 20th attempt.

Only those who do not mind making mistakes and are willing to persist until they get it right will achieve. Do you know how many times Thomas Edison tried before he finally discovered the incandescent light? Go and find out and you will discover the master of all times in mistakes. You will be amazed to know how many times he missed it before he finally got it right. What is called mistake is a step in the direction of something that we want to achieve. Don't allow fear to lead you to inaction.

Inaction in itself leads you to lack of

experience, because it's when you act on something that you discover whether that is the right way or one way not to do it. And you thereby gather experience along the way. Inaction will only lead you to lack of experience.

Lack of experience fosters ignorance. If you never attempt to do anything you will never discover, and if you never discover you will remain ignorant concerning that which you are supposed to do.

And ignorance breeds fear. So what happens to you? By not taking any action, you live in a vicious cycle that is difficult to break. The way to break the chain of fear and to move on to achievement is to step out and do it anyway. If you refuse to go for a job interview because you have never been to an interview before or because you don't know anything about interview, you will never know it and will not have the opportunity to get the job. But if you go to an interview, even if you make a mistake and you lose that job, you will learn from your mistakes at that interview, and the next time you go to another interview, you would have learned one more thing that will help you to perform better.

THE FEAR FACTOR IN BUSINESS

Always remember this:

Fear breeds Inaction,
Inaction leads to Lack of Experience,
Lack of Experience fosters Ignorance; and
Ignorance breeds Fear.
It's a cycle. You just have to cut it in the middle and go on with your life.

Some other ways fear can manifest in us are:

Procrastination

When you have fears, you will procrastinate. You will keep postponing things until tomorrow. And when that tomorrow comes it becomes another tomorrow. And since tomorrow never ends, soon enough one tomorrow will be the last day of your life and you will still not have done what you are supposed to do.

Now is the best time to act. Break the chain of fear, move forward, and do what you need to do. The bible says, "They that know their God will be strong and do exploits." Knowing God gives you confidence to move forward. Even if you make a mistake, as long as you know that God is with you, there is something in the process of that mistake that will contribute to your future. And it takes boldness and confidence to step out and do whatever you need to do.

Sluggishness
Fear will result in sluggishness because if you are afraid to take a step, you will keep hesitating, going forward and coming back, and you will never attain anything.

Not Taking Initiative
When you are afraid, you will not take initiative. You will not want to take a risk. Fearful people are not risk-takers. They are not willing to take any chance or make any move. One plus one is two in every normal sense, but the bible says one plus one equals to one. The only time you will ever discover that one plus one is one is if you get married. But if you say to yourself, "Every marriage I know is in trouble, therefore I'm never going to get married." "I'm afraid that if I get married I'm going to have an unhappy marriage myself."

This posture will only rob you of the discovery that you could have had a blissful home by marrying the right person and gaining the knowledge that you need to make sure your home is successful.

Indecision
Fear will result in indecision. If you are afraid, you will never decide one way or the other. You will keep procrastinating, you will get sluggish, at the end of the day inaction will set in. And if you don't act, you don't get results and you cannot achieve.

Fear is real for many people, but only those who have allowed themselves not to seek the knowledge they need to overcome fear. Fear can be managed and overcome. God has given you the power to do it.

Other effects of fear are:
- Timidity
- Introversion
- Reticence
- Inactivity

Do not let fear deny you of attaining your best in life. Face your fear squarely and you will be amazed at how much strength you have in you or how little there is to what you fear.

4

PARTNERSHIP

In this chapter, we are going to consider a topic that is very contentious among many people in business: Partnership. We shall look at Partnership as a way of starting a business or raising funds for one.

Most of the time, some people have great business ideas, but they don't have the necessary capital to transform these ideas into a business venture. And because of this, the tendency is for the person to be so exuberant about bringing his idea to a reality that he will be quick to jump into partnership with anyone who offers financial help, with the hope that they will work things out later.

Going by records, partnership is one dangerous form of business to just jump into. There are many sad stories that people who have blindly gone into it have had to tell at the end of it. And the causes of most of these tales of woes are issues that could have been avoided if they had only taken the time to address relevant issues before starting the partnership.

ISSUES IN PARTNERSHIP

The first question to ask is 'is it even scriptural to go into partnership?'

People are usually quick to say that the Bible says 'we should not be unequally yoked with unbelievers'. But note that the Bible does not say we should not be yoked at all with people. This means that when you decide that you are entering a business partnership with someone, the kind of considerations you would take into cognizance before going into a marriage partnership are the same you will need to note before going into the partnership.

This is because, in a legal sense, the two of you in the partnership will become one with equal

PARTNERSHIP

responsibility for your individual actions. This means that if your partner takes an action in the name of the partnership, he is acting on your behalf as well.

The problem these days is that many people jump into partnership with unequal footing. Granted that you are the one with the idea, and the other person the one with the money, both of you will still have to determine who has controlling power in the business; what your personal obligations and responsibilities are, and at what point do they end?

Here are some other important issues you need to resolve before going into partnership with anybody:
1. Under what terms or condition are you coming together as partners?
2. Who is in charge of management?
3. Who takes decisions?
4. What are the processes for taking decisions?
5. Can the financial partner come in and dictate terms?
6. Can you employ your relatives? Can you employ any of your spouses?
7. If he dies, what happens to his part in the

business?
8. If when starting the business you both were singles, then in the course of time you both get married, how does that affect your partnership?
9. Will you, as a managing partner, earn the kind of salary you would have given to an outsider if you were to employ him to run the business?
10. What are the values you both are bringing to the table to enhance the business?
11. How much interference are you going to allow?

These are some of the issues that have wrecked havocs in partnership relationships. Yet, you may discover that there are things you want to do, but which you are not able to do all by yourself; therefore necessitating that you team up with others to achieve the dream. The truth is there is value in other people being added to you. The Bible says "Two are better than one, because they have a good reward for their labour" (Ecclesiastes 4:9)

Remember we mentioned the safety that is in counsel in the previous chapter; it's the same thing with partnership. There are values that different

PARTNERSHIP

people with different skills can bring to the table, and by all means they should be exploited. But most times, we don't bother to do the due diligence of taking care of all the details that can become contentious in future before we jump into a partnership venture.

What are the core values on which the partnership will be based? If you are both Christians, are you going to agree to use the business for evangelism or not? What are you going to do with your resources? Are you going to pay tithe? Are you going to give to the work of God? If both of you go to different churches, whose church will you pay tithe to? How much would you sow into one church as opposed to the other? What's the maximum seed you can sow from the business in any given calendar year?

What kind of teachings are you going to adopt in running the business? Are you willing to be accountable to each other or choose an outsider as an arbitrator between the two of you, so that if there is any issue you go to the person you have both appointed to arbitrate? Will the person be your pastor or his pastor?

These are some of the things you need to discuss and resolve together. Let me share with you the words of Harvey Firestone of *Firestone Tires*, he says:

If the organizers of a corporation cannot agree at the beginning, there is small chance that they will afterward.

A lot of us tend to say that we will solve the problem as we go along. My answer is capital NO. Things usually get more complex when money starts flowing in. It is easier to ask every question, every thought, and anything that crosses your mind and be open with each other when you are still at level zero than when things have started to blossom. So deal with every grey issue as they arise now, rather than wait till later.

The fact that someone has the money and you have the skill does not make you a lesser partner in the business. Most people tend to trade off their skills for the person who has the money by making him a higher partner. Then they later despise him when they realize that they are the one who is actually doing most of the work.

It is also important to note that while the skilled partner is the operator who does the work, without the money of the financial partner the business might not have taken off. Therefore, it is

PARTNERSHIP

necessary to respect one another and value what each of you is bringing to the table.

Now to the person who has the money, if you are about to go into a partnership with any person, never take advantage of him because he has no money. He might seem handicapped because he has the skills and a desire to bring something to pass, but doesn't have the money to start off. And in most cases, most people who have the skills are willing to lick your boot in order to get the money to go ahead with his project. But some time later, when the business is running smoothly, they may look back and begin to feel cheated when they consider some of the terms of the partnership.

As the financial partner, you will be justified in such cases because you both agreed to the terms before starting the venture. But in your own interest, you should ensure that you are fair in all situations. You need your partner to always be in a positive state of mind, so that he can give his best to the business. The truth is, if he is not happy and he is able to make enough money from the business, he can pull out and go to start all over on his own, and if he is good enough, he will succeed again.

When there is a challenge in a business, it is

easier for the operating partner to understand it because he is directly involved in the day-to-day running of the operations, but the financial partner usually finds it difficult to understand because his reason for investing in the venture is to make financial returns. This underscores the fact that two people going into business together does not mean that they have the same reason for going into the business.

The partner who is the technical person wants to build his dream. He has a desire to build an institution; something he can call his own. It is not as if he does not want to make money; but the joy of setting up a business, by building it from the scratch to the top, is usually more important to him than the money. He is more than willing to make sacrifices and even sell at a lower profit margin in order to gain more customers. But the financial person, on the other hand, has another motive for buying into the dream and may not see things from the entrepreneur's view.

This is why you should always discuss issues. You might assume both of you want the same thing, but a lot of times that is not the case. The financial partner may just be interested in returns

PARTNERSHIP

for his investment. And whereas the operator is willing to wait for longer-term profit, he is more short-term oriented.

How then do you reconcile this? The Bible asks, "Can two walk together except they agree"? (Amos 3:3). If you don't have agreement right from the beginning of the venture, you are setting up for failure. That is why it's important that you both sit together from the outset and agree on key terms.

Let's look at the case of two single young men who came into partnership together. And after some time they both got married. Now you might like the person you went into partnership with, but that doesn't mean that you will like his choice of wife. And while he is going to become one with his wife, and you become one with yours as well, both of you are also one in business!

Now which oneness will supersede the other? The covenant of marriage is a divine one, which no one should go against, but at the same time, the business covenant that brings you together has a legal backing as well. Soon enough, your wife and your partner's wife's opinion will start to influence the decisions you make in life. How will you resolve that?

What happens if any of the partners drop dead? If your partnership agreement is not well stated to include that if one of the partners dies the other person buys out his shares, that means your partner's wife automatically becomes your partner! Is that the partner you chose when you started the business?

There is a tendency for most Christians to assume that because the other person is a Christian, then they have fulfilled the "being equally yoked" condition in the Bible, and therefore can go into business together. This is not a good enough basis for partnership. It can only be good if the other person, although a Christian, is an ideal match for you to do business with: that is you share the same vision, the same dream, and both your long and short-term goals are the same etc.

The area of goals is usually problematic. While both your short-term goals may be similar, that is to set up a business; your long-term goals may be different. Your own long-term goal may be to build a business you will sell off in some years' time to make some money, while your partner may have no interest whatsoever in selling, but may derive great pleasure in the existence of a company

PARTNERSHIP

bearing his name. He may even have a plan to train one of his children to take up the business after him.

That is a legitimate dream, as long as it is what he wants. But if what you want is a business that you can sell off at a good value ten years later, that is legitimate for you as well. But this means you both will be heading towards two different directions even though you started at the same point.

There have been many bitter ends to a lot of partnerships. So, it's important that you take the time to sort out all the details. Take time to agree on what your short-term and long-term goals are. Agree on conditions that if you get to a point when you two no longer agree, how will you dissolve the relationship: what role would your spouses play? What role would your pastors play? Do you have a right to go to your pastor and report your partner, or do you go to an independent arbitrator who is neutral and not related to any of you?

Though partnership is an easy way to raise money or get the additional skills needed to start a business, there are a lot of issues attached to it. I want you to consider it as one of the biggest decisions you will ever make in your business life, and don't be quick to jump into it.

That is not to say that partnership does not work. There are many successful partnerships around, but success can only come when you have taken the time to iron out where you are going, the terms of the relationship, the season of review, among others. You can agree that at the end of every two years you will sit down and review the basis of your relationship, and at each time decide on the terms to move forward, with the power of arbitration always acknowledged in your agreement. So that when disagreement comes, you have already resolved, in advance, how it would be solved without any form of bitterness.

There is so much to partnership that it cannot be exhausted here. But as questions keep coming up in your mind, do not hesitate to raise them. For it is better to resolve all grey issues at the beginning than later when the business has taken off. It is even more complex when money has started coming in, because money has a way of redefining people's reaction. People tend to interpret things differently when money is involved. But when you are at level zero it is easier to smoothen out all the rough edges, real and perceived.

5

HONESTY IN BUSINESS

In this chapter, we shall look at the topic **HONESTY IN BUSINESS,** with special focus on **PRICING.**

Honesty. That is a rare word in the marketplace today. A lot of us have taken for granted that it is okay to be as dishonest as you can be as long as no one catches you. But for those of us who profess to be Christians, the Bible says that we shall be known by our fruits. Can we then afford to be dishonest? Can we project the image of Christ, who we are supposed to represent in our businesses, by being dishonest? Can we afford to go into business with people and leave them with an impression that we are neither honest nor trustworthy because of the way we conduct our transactions?

The Bible says, *"The crooked man is an abomination to the LORD, but He is intimate with the upright"* (Proverbs 3:32). The truth of the matter is that we cannot experience intimacy with God when we are dishonest. And if this be the case, how can you pray to God to bless your business or call upon Him when you have challenges in your business?

The primary reason we are in business, as Christians, is to represent Christ; so that people might see Him in our conducts. It therefore behoves us to be honest in everyone of our dealings in the business place. The Bible says, *"The love of money is the root of all evil"* (1 Timothy 6:10). Money in itself is not evil, but it is the inordinate way we seek it that makes us disregard every value held dear by God.

How far can you go in the marketplace if the people you deal with do not believe whatever you say? Dishonesty makes transactions difficult and increases the cost of doing business. Because we do not trust each other, we always have to involve lawyers in every little thing we do; we document every detail and write and re-write agreement to secure ourselves from being cheated, whereas in the olden days, a simple handshake would have sealed the transaction.

Talking about pricing, the Bible says in Proverbs 16:11 that *"A just weight and balance are the LORD'S: all the weights of the bag are his concern."* What this means is that it is important to God that our scales are just in all our transactions, and that we deal with every man in openness and truth. The Bible also says, *"A good name is rather to be chosen than great riches, and loving favour rather than silver and gold"* (Proverbs 22:1).

If you choose to do things in the way of God, and you build a business that is based on integrity and character, people will come to recognise you for what you stand for and they will definitely seek you out wherever you may be, though this may take a while.

Sometimes it seems that those who are doing things the 'fast way' are the ones that prosper more than the righteous ones. But I assure you that the little that the righteous has is always far more beneficial than the wealth of the wicked (Proverbs 16:8). The Bible compares the wealth of the wicked to grass, which rises quickly, but after a while is cut off, withers, and a fire is set on it. While the wealth of the righteous is a like a palm tree, which stands for all seasons and times (Psalm 92:7,12). The kind of wealth you want is the one that will give you peace of mind and maintains your testimony, not the type that will bring you sorrow and restlessness.

You are supposed to price your goods with the principle of fairness. Take cognizance of all your expenses; the costs of your goods, and other running costs. Add it all up and add whatever you consider a reasonable profit to it without exploiting the buyers. Sometimes the forces of the market dictate its own price, which you can do nothing about; a case of scarcity could make the price of your goods go up so that you make a great profit from your sales. That is fine, as long as your intention is not to cheat or take undue advantage of your customers.

LEGITIMATE REASONS FOR DIFFERING PRICES

You may wonder if there are legitimate cases where your price can be different from one transaction to another. Yes, there are a few situations where you can charge different prices. And we shall consider some of them below.

VOLUME/BULK DISCOUNT

If you are selling and you decide to offer a special discount to anyone who buys large quantities of your products, that is a legitimate reason for price difference. What is important is that such offer must be applicable to all. In other words, if the person who buys ten units today decides to buy hundred tomorrow you will offer him the same treatment.

The Bible states that we must deal with all men in fairness and sincerity. And not use different rules or measure for any, nor sell for one person at a higher price because you perceive that he is rich, and then sell for another person at a lower price because he looks poor. That is what is called a 'differing measure'. It is not acceptable in the eyes of God.

CASH DISCOUNT

You can also offer what is called Cash Discount. This is done by giving a certain percentage of cash discount to those that come to your shop to buy your goods within a specified time. Even if it is transactions with companies where you send them invoice, you could choose to say that those that make their payment in ten days will get a certain discount.

This is another legitimate reason to have different prices, and if anyone decides to take you up on it, you can easily explain yourself and even offer the same facility to him if he or she is able to meet the requirement.

CLASS DISCOUNT

You can also have a class discount. You could decide, as a business policy or out of the goodness of your heart, that when older people come to buy, you will give them discount. Perhaps because you recognize that they are pensioners who do not have much, and you want to create some value for them.

The price that you sell ordinarily should be the true value of the product. Except for specific reasons, you cannot afford to apply different principles to different people with an intention of taking advantage of one person over another. The Bible teaches that we be honest with all men, and be fair in all we do. And when pricing a product, you should charge the right price for the right product.

You don't want to be like one of my brothers who would put the label of SONY or TOSHIBA on a gadget that originally has no label, and then offer this product for customers at the price of the original one. This is outright cheating and dishonesty. The seed we sow today are always waiting down the road for us; and we will definitely reap our harvest.

There is a longer time value inherent in you seeking to do the right things with all men; irrespective of whom they are or where they come from. Imagine if God deals with us based on our race or nature, how many of us would qualify for His mercy, His love and His grace?

As God is honest and sincere with all men, so does He require that in all our dealings we should be honest, sincere and truthful with one another. He detests a double-dealer (Proverbs 6:16-17). And if you make yourself detestable to God it means that you cannot go into His presence to ask for His help or anything else for that matter. And when the going gets tough or all that you think you have acquired just disappears one day, who will you call for help?

6

BUSINESS BONDAGE

In this chapter, we shall consider another interesting topic, BUSINESS BONDAGE. You might wonder what Business Bondage is. There are many people in business who ordinarily appear to be free agents, but who are in bondage in actuality. They are in bondage to their business; in bondage to their dreams; in bondage to their drive for success; in bondage to work of any kind; or in bondage to the system. There are many issues attached to business bondage, and some of them we will consider below.

There are a lot of family men who had set out to succeed in business, but who have lost everything else in the process. The wife is gone because the man is never there for her. The children are all over the place doing whatever they like because the man is no longer there to provide discipline and balance. Competition has set into the home, but in this case it is the business that is competing with the family for the man's attention.

A man leaves his house as early as 6.00am and does not get back until about 11.00pm. Or in the case of those who seek political positions, they spend the whole day out and most of the night as well, because the kind of meeting they do could only hold in the wee hours of the day.

There are different kinds of bondage on the side of the man or the woman. Moreover, there are many women as well who, because of the pursuit of their career and the drive to succeed, have had to sacrifice everything else. Sometimes maybe because of the mindset that 'I'm a woman, and to succeed I have to do as much as a man.' We work beyond the point that makes sense for us as a woman who has other responsibilities in her life. We sacrifice our husbands and children. My question is that at the end of the day what will we hold on to if we've lost everything in the drive to achieve what we're seeking? Business bondage is a real issue, and a BIG ISSUE!!!

Some are in bondage to the system. How can one be in bondage to the system? If even as a Christian because you are seeking to succeed you have decided that the only way things can be done here is to follow the way every other person does it. How does every body else does it? When you need to get a job in a place, you already have a pre-arrangement that says you will get every LPO that gets out of this company. But you know that out of everything that is going to come out certain percentage will go to the person on the seat, you are in bondage to the system. The word of God becomes forsaken in your life because of your drive to achieve success. And you can't break away because you think that you can't succeed outside the system. And so you remain in that imprisonment of your drives and your dreams.

Sometimes we are in bondage even to our ambitions. A man with a political ambition will do things that ordinarily he would never do. We all know the sagas of "Okija" that made the headlines a little while ago on the things people do either for business or career. When men would stoop so low as to go in pursuit of the kind of powers that they cannot even deliver themselves from later on. But because they think that they have no option and there is no other way they can succeed they are in bondage to their career, they are in bondage to their drive, they are in bondage to their dreams, and every other thing has to wait.

There are women who are in bondage to their career as well. And because of this they would sleep with their bosses, they have lost sight of what is important and concluded that the most important thing is that they are able to get to the next step of the corporate ladder, and if what they have to do to get there is to sleep with the man, then so be it. Better get it over with and forget it. That is when you get to hear the saying that 'a man has got to do what he's got to do.' That is a lie from hell! Because a man has got to do what God wants him to do, and yet he will succeed.

Can any man prosper except the LORD allows him? The Bible says that except the LORD builds a house, the labourers labour only in vain and that the watchmen stay awake for nothing if the LORD doesn't watch over a city (Psalm 127:1-2). So to assume that it is only by sticking to certain processes or procedures that men have devised in order to get to where you are heading is a betrayal of your ignorance of who you really are. It is not to know who God is in your life; it also shows that you really do not know who control all things.

The Bible says that God rules in the affairs of men (Daniel 4:17). Men don't rule in their own affairs. Even when a man is boss over you, he is only boss over you because God has allowed him to, which is why the Bible says that we must submit to the authorities in our lives. As long as you are under that man you will do what he says you should do as long as it is in line with the word of God. Business bondage is a real issue.

What about overwork? There are some men who are totally consumed with their work at the expense of anything else. Why do they work so hard? Because they think that it is only by working so hard that they can prosper. They forget the passage that says: "it is vain for you to rise up early, to sit up late, to eat the bread of sorrow, for so He gives His beloved sleep." (Psalm 127:2). Even while you are sleeping God can bless you.

BUSINESS HIS WAY

There is a portion of the bible that says "your gates shall be continually open, it shall not be shut day or night that men can bring you the wealth of the gentiles and their kings in procession" (Isaiah 60:11). Do you know what that means? When God says that your gates shall be continually open, He does not mean that when you open your office at 8.00 o'clock in the morning you are going to be opened till 8.00am the following morning and continue on a roller-coaster of 24-7. No! No! What He actually means is that when you work within the hours that are reasonable, assuming that is 8-6. And on a day that you need to go to church, because you need to serve God, and you work within the normal hours, and you assign the time that is God's to God and you go to seek or do the things of God. While you're busy doing the things of God and it is time to sleep, you go to sleep because your body needs that rest to continue to work, some other person who has no knowledge or understanding of God, who is totally consumed with doing things in the way of the world, will be at work for you.

Now that may be hard for some to understand. But how does it happen? Let me use myself as an example. In some cases, there are people who have different connections to get certain kinds of jobs. They go ahead to make all sort of deals. The kind of deals that I definitely will not want to make, maybe because it involves bribery or some form of cheating an organisation or the government. Now after they have stayed awake all night and expended much stress to get the job, it would so happen that they would not be able to deliver on that job, or they would not on their own have what it takes to do the job. So what are they? They are LPO merchants. When they get the documents they will seek for people like me or somebody else who have chosen to do things God's way. And they would bring that order that they have stayed awake all night to get for me to supply.

And in delivering on that job, assuming that it is a government contract, they would have to first pay me for me to deliver on it. And when they pay me I will be blessed by the transaction. Now they might sometimes have to wait for as long as it takes, at times for months or even sometimes years, before they get paid by the organisation or the government agency. We all read in the newspapers of companies that have qualified under the due diligence process to collect payments for jobs that were probably done years ago. And if they had given the job to somebody like me to execute, they probably must have already paid me, so the loss is theirs.

While I was sleeping, they were awake making a deal and getting the job in the middle of the night. And in the morning when I wake up afresh, having followed my God and His will, they would need what I have to deliver on their deals. The Bible says 'as many as are led by the spirit of God are the sons of God' (Romans 8: 14). God in leading me will make sure that I already have the products they needed in stock, or I would have ordered for it. So they come to me, and I take the job and benefit from their sleeplessness and stress. That is how your gates can be continually open, and will not be shut day or night because there are people who are working on your behalf while you are fast asleep. The last part of that scripture says, "For men to bring to you the wealth of the gentiles." Who are the gentiles? They are unbelievers; they are people who are willing to do things their own way and not God's way, and while they are doing that you get blessed by it.

BUSINESS BONDAGE

No man can prosper by his own sweat. You can work very hard. The simplest example I can give you is if you go to a construction site and see the labour. The men who are involved in the process of casting the foundation and the pillar, they are the ones that work. They carry this pan of heavy concrete up and down different heights, sweating it out with a lot of energy. How much is involved in that work? Or you go to a place like Oshodi and you see the women that are sitting by the roadside even at 12 midnight with a tray of wares that may not be more than N2000 to N5000, and they are still trying to make the next sale of N10 or N30 even at that hour! And you see an innocent little child sleeping beside them in the open space and a chilly weather; that is work!

But a man cannot only prosper by mere work. The Bible says that 'if a man does not work he shouldn't eat' (2 Thessalonians 3:10). So this is not encouraging you to be lazy, but what I am saying is that it is God who prospers your work and turns it to success. It is not a matter of how hard you work.

So when we become so consumed with work, we inadvertently get into bondage by losing sight of everything else, and by sacrificing our families and loved ones. Then there will be no time to serve or worship God, there will be no time to benefit even our fellow men. Have you checked the obituary pages of the newspapers recently? There are too many people dying at very early age, cases abound of many young people who just collapsed and died because of keeping late nights, late afternoons, travelling back and forth and running in circles to gain one contract or another. And then just as he gets the contract, he drops dead. What happens thereafter? Someone he does not reckon with in his lifetime will be the one to benefit from all the money he leaves behind.

Everything we do in life needs a balance. Larry Burkett, a business minister who has invested over 30 years developing biblical principles for business, says "No one can maintain the correct balance between business, family and God if he or she is working more than 60 hours per week." And the truth is that some people work longer than this, sleeping between four to five hours, going round the bend from day to day, Monday to Sunday. They don't even know which day is Saturday and which is Sunday. Any day is good for a meeting or an appointment. Any moment is perfect for everything business.

Such people are not different from a prisoner. In fact the person in prison is probably better off. The only luxury they have above prisoners is that they get to choose the clothes they wear and can afford fancy clothes. And perhaps they have a driver who probably has a better life than they do, because all the time when they are running around for meetings, the driver would probably recline on the seat of the fancy car, puts on the AC and goes to sleep while the boss is under stress at work.

I will like to look at another aspect of work bondage. I want to look at holidays and the impact of work bondage on it. I'm sure there are many of you who have not taken a vacation for a very long time. You are entitled to annual leave. Your employers have provided for an annual leave because your body is not a machine. It cannot work non-stop forever. But some people would rather trade off their vacation for money without any consideration of the fact that they need to rest. And apart from that, without even considering that by going on vacation, they have a little more time to spend with their family.

Sometimes, we are the ones really serving the people around us, whom we think are at our service. If your work starts at 8.00am, get there on time, do the things you need to do at the right hours; granted there will be occasions when you need to work late, but if it becomes an everyday practice, then something is wrong. There are bosses who will keep their workers at work till 9.00pm or 10:00pm because their people cannot leave until they leave.

I know people who have chosen to go for lower-paying jobs in order to maintain their sanity and fulfil their responsibilities to themselves and their loved ones. I think the sector that is probably most guilty of this sin is the banking industry at a certain era. They seem to have improved a lot now, but it was most disastrous for many women who found themselves there. There were some I counselled with who at the end of the day had to define and make a choice between life and imprisonment, bondage or freedom.

The Bible says that "he whom the Son has set free is free indeed" (John 8:36). How can you be proclaimed free and of your own accord went ahead to sign yourself into the prison of your work bondage? Think about it. There are so much more to life.

When was the last time you went to dinner with your wife or took your children out? You don't even have the time. There are people whose mobile phones will ring at 3.00am and they will wake to pick it up. That is another one. Phones have become a source of bondage to a lot of people. Someone once told me that their boss presented all his staff with a mobile phone each when it first came out so that he would be able to reach them whenever he wanted, which is any hour of the day. And imagine, they had received calls from him at odd hours like 1.00am or 6.00am!

There was a day a certain gentleman we were doing business with called me at an unearthly hour and I was so irritated. For some reason I forgot to switch off my phone the previous night and when his call came in, I panicked that maybe someone had an emergency and so quickly got up to pick the phone. Imagine my annoyance when it turned out to be a normal business call. I did not waste time to tell him my mind, and he was so full of apology saying that his MD had called him several times in the last one hour to give him a feedback on the transaction. I told him if I were his wife I would have thrown his phone in the gutter because that means he doesn't have a life.

He was probably at the office the day before till about 10pm. That is not life. That is bondage and imprisonment. An invisible prison has been created in the workplace and so we do not have time for God or the systems that He has created around us in order to make our life balanced and allow His purpose to be manifested in us.

How can you even think? A lot of people have become monsters. They react out of place in certain situations due to the pressure of work. So who suffers? Everyone around them do. But it is high time we looked at it and decide what is really important. And determine if it is worth all the stress or not. At the end of the day you will be tired and exhausted, and you will look back and ask yourself where have all the years gone?

I am asking you to think about it now and don't wait till the end. Is it worth it to sign yourself into the prison yard of your business, of your career, or whatever it is that is taking the greatest chunk of your time at the expense of things that really matter? Search for the balance. The Bible says, 'it is neither by power, nor by might but by My spirit, says the LORD' (Zechariah 4:6). Only God can bless you. Yes, you should be diligent, you should be painstaking, and you should do everything that needs to be done. But you should also do all within the limit of balance, and don't ignore God.

The Bible says, 'seek first the kingdom of God, and every other thing will be added to you' (Matthew 6:33). When you seek God first, you won't need overnight meetings to get contracts. Since 'the steps of the righteous are ordered by the LORD'. He will order your steps in the right direction, to the right place, at the right moment.

What creates success for us in business? It is being at the right place at the right time for the right opportunities, as well as having the abilities to take hold of those opportunities when they appear. That is how we attain business success. Now, who can orchestrate those things? It is no other person but God! He is the one that has control of the hearts of men.

You might have done all you ordinarily

should do, but what happens if the man you have been spending sleepless nights with in meetings suddenly drops dead on the morning he is to sign the contract deal? And somebody else takes over his position and you have to start all over again? And the new person probably has his own interests and his own person for the job as well. What will you do then?

God is the one who can give you supernatural favour that will make even your enemies become your friends. The bible says 'all things work together for good for those who love God and are the called according to His purpose' (Romans 8:28). Are you called according to the purpose of God? Are you seeking the purpose of God or your own personal agenda? Are you doing it by your own power and strength? Your strength will fail. You can only go so far. Your trust in man will fail, but your trust in God will produce the man that will bless you. Your seeking God will produce the right opportunity for you at the right time in the right place.

Work bondage is real and a lot of people are caught in it. Let us continually examine ourselves and check to see that we are not caught in its web.

BUSINESS BONDAGE

Let us consider the things that are important to God. Your family is important to God because He made you an ambassador in that house to raise those children for Him and to nurture your wife to her full potential.

If you are a woman, God gave you the calling of a mother, the responsibility to nurture your children and to be a helpmate to your husband. If in bondage to your work you failed in all of those, you will be answerable to Him, and He will not accept excuses. You cannot tell God "the reason I was not able to raise those children was because I also have to work." No. No. He has given you the ability and wisdom to succeed in your calling, e.g in your career, as a wife and a mother. And one will not be accepted as an excuse for failure in another.

You are meant to succeed in all three offices. You are meant to succeed as a wife, as a mother, and in your career or business or whatever God has called you to. It is your responsibility to seek the balance that will give you that success. If you are in a place that does not provide that environment, that is another thing.

Money is another major source of our bondage. Because you get certain kind of salary in some places, whereas you know that environment cannot allow you to fulfil your assignment and purpose in life, you don't want to leave because you don't want to lose the money. But the truth is, money is such an insignificant factor, because if you are hungry and you have a house filled with money you cannot eat it, if there is no food. If you were naked and you needed clothes, you cannot stitch your money together and wear it as a garment. People will strip you off it in seconds on the street. So the real value of money is what you can do with it. Do not allow the money that you are likely to get from a contract, or the salary you get from a place to be the reason that you will be in bondage to that place, to that work, or to that contract.

Some women cannot say No because of the things they benefit from their office. Why would you sell off the greatest thing that God gave you as a woman because of some miserable job, no matter how much money it offers? A day will come when you will not be attractive any more. God is the centre of our life and everything that we do we must do it to honour Him. We must seek His purpose and seek to fulfil His plan. And if we allow ourselves to be in bondage to anything that will distract us from that which God has called us to do, then we have failed. Bondage is real in our career, business and the workplace.

There are times that you don't even know some things about your children except you are around them at certain hours of the day. It is easy for a child to say "good morning daddy" with a nice, innocent smile when daddy is going out in the morning. It is also easy for the child to do whatever and be back before 9.00pm if she knows that daddy gets home at nine, and she still looks so innocent and sweet without daddy knowing what is going on. Some that are even affluent, when their kids are in the study and are sitting on the internet don't know what is going on or what they are looking at on the internet. There is so much garbage out there and many things going on that we can't afford to shirk our responsibilities as parents.

There are husbands whose wives are getting attention from other places, because they are never on ground to appreciate what they have themselves. You need to be around your family. You are not even there at weekends!

Create time to take a holiday with your family; you can travel with your children. And travelling doesn't really mean going abroad. So don't say 'I can't afford it.' You can go to your village or another town, a place where you have no commitment and no one looks for you. Sleep; hang around your children and the little things that you would learn about them will make a world of difference in your relationship with them. You would have time to seek the face of God, pray, get a direction for your life, and to think about other issues. We are products of the decisions we make on a day-to-day basis. But if we don't even position ourselves in a setting to make the right kind of decision we will only end up in trouble.

Holidays afford us the time to look back and see things with a clearer mind, so we are able to take better decisions. Even during the Christmas season, there are people who do not take a break except on the Christmas day itself when no office is open. Mind you, some people are always ready to open their office even on Christmas day if they think some business can be done that day! Some even consider the New Year day a business day!

BUSINESS BONDAGE

This is not good enough. Enjoy the other things of life. Life is so called because it is full of many things that keep one alive.

Work in itself can drown you if you are so obsessed with it. There is someone I respect so much, who is the managing director of one of the banks. He gets to his desk very early in the morning, but by 6.00pm he is on his way home to his family. You could get to his house on a Saturday and you would see him lying on the couch reading a book. He is around his children. He has time to sit down and have a chat with his wife. He is not a stranger in his home.

You can have it all. So why choose to have just one of the all? Because if all you have is your work you have only just one of them. There is so much more to life

7

BRIBERY & CORRUPTION

The issue we shall discuss in this chapter is a very controversial one indeed; it is titled Corruption. We shall be considering bribery as an aspect of corruption. Bribery seems to be at the central point of corruption and is one can of worms that has been unleashed on our dear country, Nigeria. And no matter how much we have tried, we have not been able to gather the worms back into the can and seal it up.

A report released by Transparency International some time ago adjudged Nigeria as the third most corrupt nation in the world. One of the most embarrassing moments I usually have in business is sitting at a table with some organisation abroad trying to discuss serious issues, and someone comes across to you with perceived mistrust or an assumption that because you are a Nigerian or you are representing a Nigerian company, you are likely to have those dubious characteristics that the people have come to be associated with. We all suffer this embarrassment in many ways and under many conditions. And I, like many other Nigerians, am sick of answering for the actions and activities of those who have refused to be true Nigerians or present our country as it really is.

I am writing with a lot of conviction because I know that the way we are portrayed by the international media is not true. I know there are many Nigerians who deal without bribery and are still very successful. I have also found in my experience as a businessperson that there are enough corporate organisations in this country with decent staffs who are committed to representing their companies with integrity and character; who deal basically on merit, performance and track record; and will not compromise their position because of a bribe.

You will be surprised to know the number of passages condemning bribery in the Bible. And it scares me as a person to see that people will know God's position on such a matter and are still able to go to bed at night after collecting or giving a bribe! When it comes to bribery, it involves two people. If one wants to take and the other isn't willing to give, nobody will be able to take. So the giver and the taker are both guilty in the matter.

I hear everyday in the media that our president said he is trying to rid the country of corruption; it is only when Nigerians themselves are committed to making our country corruption-free by not paying bribes or indulging in other corrupt practices will that ever happen. The president is not going to come to your office to ask or represent you. He is not going to sit in the office of every one of his ministers or every public officer. We are the ones that can make the needed difference. When you and I refuse to give or ask for a bribe, then we can have a chance to change what this country will become.

I'm a woman of faith. I strongly believe a day will come when every Nigerian will proudly be able to hold their heads high for the integrity and character our country will be known by, as reflected in our individual behaviours. And if we Christians become fully committed to this ideal, there is no way we will not affect our society for good and spice it positively like the salt that the Bible says we are; thus, we will begin the necessary change process.

One person can begin a change process. Revival is what we need where bribery and corruption are concerned. And revival needs just one person who is committed, and that one person should be you. When you are committed, I am committed, and one other person is committed, we begin a chain of righteousness, and soon enough we will create a new order with a bribe-free environment rather than one that is totally sold out on bribery.

I am going to cite a lot of Bible references in this discourse because I want you to know and appreciate the extent to which God hates and detests the act of bribery. And for you to appreciate what really happens when someone builds a corruption-ridden life that men perceive as prosperous. What that person is really doing is pouring petrol on the house he has built; the petrol in this instance represents the bribe he is collecting. And at the end of the day he will, with his own hand, strike a match and throw it at the house and it will be totally consumed in destruction. That is the implication of what the Bible says when one sits comfortably in the place of bribery and feeds fat on the seed of corruption.

In Exodus 23:8, the Bible says, *"And you shall not take a bribe: for a bribe blinds the clear-sighted, and subverts the cause of the just."*

God is the just one. In this passage He was giving specific instruction to the children of Israel on how to relate to one another. We are the spiritual Israel of today, having being ransomed by the blood of Jesus. And He is saying to us here that once you collect a bribe, you become a blind man. What do you think will happen to a blind man? Even though he walks as though he has sight, eventually he will end up in a ditch. What does a ditch represent? It represents a place of destruction. That is why you can see a government official or the purchasing officer of some company who has made a lot of money for himself through bribery, built a magnificent house, and for some mysterious reason the house caught fire and is totally destroyed! Or even in a situation where this is not the case, he is told one day that his child, on whom he had spent so much money of the stolen money to sponsor to one of the best schools in America, has lost his mind. Because he has a lot of money from his father's stolen wealth and is able to buy drugs, and so becomes a drug addict. And one day something goes wrong and he becomes an inmate at the asylum.

Such a man, because he has become blinded by bribery and is working against a just God in an unjust manner, will never find peace. Ill-gotten wealth will destroy the owner in the long run. As a blind man he will only end up in a ditch.

In Deuteronomy 27:28, God says, *"Cursed is the one who accepts to receive a bribe to strike down an innocent person. And all the people shall say Amen."*

If you are a Nigerian reading this book right now, the Bible says 'there is power of life and death in the tongue' (Proverbs 18:21). Because you and I want to get a fair deal and treatment in every situation; and do not want to be cheated or

BRIBERY & CORRUPTION

disallowed from what we are qualified for or able to do; and because we do not want to continue to apologise for the ills of other people, you and I can pronounce together upon those that are working against our country, just as God has pronounced against them. Therefore you and I shall say 'Amen' to the pronouncement above. Because it is the Word of God and we are pronouncing it upon every individual that is destroying the image of our country or working against its development.

The money that is meant for the repair of our roads, our hospitals, usually ends up in some people's pockets; the drugs that are meant to save lives are either diverted and sold elsewhere, or somebody somewhere is taking a bribe and is allowing dangerous and expired drugs into the country to be distributed to innocent people, and many have died in the process. Thank God for a woman like Dr Dora Akunyili, the Director General of NAFDAC, who has made so much difference in our health sector. It doesn't matter how many people are after her life, they will never catch up with her because God is always protecting the righteous.

We are going to say this together, we will

pronounce a word and we know that it will come to pass because God has spoken it, we are in agreement with Him, and His word stands sure forever: *"Cursed is the one who accepts to receive a bribe to strike down an innocent person. And all the people shall say Amen."* (Deuteronomy 27:28).

The policeman who takes a bribe from a rich man and helps him to jail an innocent person, or who helps a criminal to escape justice, is cursed according to the word of God. So when something evil happens to him he should not say it is his stepmother or his people in the village that are responsible. He shouldn't say it is because of some generational curse in his family that things are going wrong for him. He should rather trace the source of his misfortunes to the wrong acts he commits every day. Every moment someone takes a bribe, he is heaping curses upon his head like a man who is pouring hot coals upon his own head. And who can put out such fire when it is an act of God?

Bribery is a deadly indulgence. It is no different from taking a cobra and with one's own hand and bringing it into his house to sleep on his bed! Because one day that cobra will raise its head and strike, and what that means is sudden death and destruction.

I am here challenging a practice that we have assumed and accepted to be a normal way of life. It cannot be. For as long as it is against the word of God it is not possible for it to be a norm. We have to break the hold of the enemy upon this country. I want to be able, like many Nigerians, to compete in an even environment. I want a situation where a young man who doesn't have a parent with any high-power connection, but who is qualified for whatever he wants to do, to bid on a level ground. And if at the end of the day he doesn't get it then he can walk away with the mind that he at least had a fair chance to compete, and was not ousted because someone subverted the course of justice.

Another thing is that we Nigerians lose out on many fronts and foreigners benefit where we should, because our own people have collected a bribe from them to give the meat that belongs to the children of the house to strange people who came from outside. It is not done anywhere in the world. And I am here confessing and hoping that there are other people who are in agreement with me that in our lifetime, we will see a country that we dream our country to be.

And don't say it is impossible, it is very possible. We only need to believe in it, walk in it, and you and I make a commitment to live our lives that way. Even if you are the only person, let people abuse you all round; let them call you a fool, you stay committed to it. I have been called a fool many times for not doing business the general way. I can stand today and confidently say that I will walk away from any job that involves bribery without any sense of loss. This is because I know that the Bible says *"Righteousness exalts a nation, but sin is a reproach to any person"* (Proverbs 14:34). When your wealth is based on righteousness, you would have peace, joy and an inheritance to leave for your children. You will be sure that when destruction comes, it will pass over you as it passed over the children of Israel on the day of Passover.

It doesn't matter if our governors and our senators are taking bribes and stealing all our money. It doesn't matter if other people who are sitting in public offices are taking bribe to pervert the course of justice. How much can a man spend?

BRIBERY & CORRUPTION

How many houses can one live in at a time? How many cars can one ride? Even if he has various models of cars, he will only sit in one at a time. Even if he decides that a convoy of ten cars should go before and behind him, he can only sit in one of them. That is the futility of amassing wealth unjustly.

God is an awesome God. We have got to a point where we take Him for granted. We have absolutely no fear and do things without qualms. A young woman spoke to me once about a project she wanted to do. She was indeed qualified for the project. In fact she was recommended by an international body. And she had actually been awarded the contract by the government agency she wanted to work for until the personal assistant of the minister came to her and said the invoice must be increased so that some amount could go to the minister for his political campaign. This was the condition she had to meet to get the contract signed and paid for.

As a young woman who feared the Lord, and one who wanted to build a righteous organisation, she came for us to discuss this development and I told her to drop it. It was a very painful decision for her to take. It can be very painful to give up something you know you can do, and even do better than the person who will eventually take it, just because you don't want to pay a bribe. But you need to know that there is no man who will stand up for God and lose in the process. No, not one. It might look like you have lost for a season, but time always tells the story. And no man has control over time. If only we learn to look at things the way God sees them, then our decisions will be different.

Let me take another scripture verse, Deuteronomy 16:19-20 says, *"You shall not distort justice, you shall not be partial, and you shall not take a bribe, for a bribe blinds the eyes of the wise and perverts the words of the righteous."*

That means there are many blind people walking on our streets, sitting in our offices, in our senate, in our house of representatives, and in various government positions in our country. I guess you and I can pray that the Lord will open their eyes that they may see. And thus turn the situation of our country around for the better.

I am a very proud Nigerian. We are a great country with a great future. And God has done everything by giving us more than enough resources we can boast of. I truly love Nigeria, whenever I get into any other country and the cold wind blows on me I always remember home, and I am glad and grateful to God that He has made me a Nigerian. I hope you are too. And I am determined that your children and my children will live and grow up in a country that God has assigned them to be. We are going to close this can of worms called corruption. You and I can choose to make a difference. We can decide that today I will pick one worm of bribery and you can pick one as well and drop it back in the can.

How can we do that? Every time you say 'No' to bribery, every time you refuse to take a bribe no matter the cost to you, you are helping to fill back that can of worms. The price we pay for resisting bribery is usually temporary, the Bible says that the things we see are temporary, and those we do not see are the eternal ones. The eternal things do not mean that it is only when we get to heaven that we will get them. We have the heavenly rewards for sure, but there is a lot of reward that we get here on earth, one of them is the fact that you can go to sleep in your house without fear of danger.

The foolishness of this whole thing about

bribery is that no matter how much you can give, there is someone else who can give more. So how far can you go because there is always somebody who is willing to pay more than you? And there will be a point when you cannot even move forward anymore. We have suffered enough because of this can of worms called bribery. I hope you and I and many more Nigerians will decide to resist it henceforth.

It is a little daunting to see the number of biblical references that address bribery and how strong the words are. I shall be taking some more scriptural references to prove this point:

In 2 Chronicles 19:7, the Bible says, *"Now therefore, let the fear of the LORD be upon you; take care and do it, for there is no iniquity with the LORD our God, no partiality or taking of bribes."*

The Bible says that we have been made in the image of God (Genesis 1:22), and we are meant to be like Him. We should live our lives aspiring to build a God-like character, because He meant that we will be like Him in every way. And if God is not partial and would not take bribe from anyone, but deals with all fairly, why then would we who are made in His image consider that we have no other way to attain prosperity except by corruption? The Bible has already told us that 'God delights in the prosperity of His people' (Psalm 35:27). But He meant for us to prosper in a certain way; a way that will glorify His name.

He said 'do unto others as you want them to do to you,' that is what is popularly called the golden rule. An act of bribery is an act for the self and against the other person. It is an indication that we are more concerned about what we get and really don't care about what happens to anybody else, including the offices where we work, the government agency we represent, the people that we are responsible to, our employers and people we are accountable to. The act of bribery is an act of selfishness and it is also destructive, because in every situation where bribery is exchanged somebody is paying the price, and it is not a price by choice, but by coercion.

Job 15:34 says, *"For the company of the hypocrites will be barren, and fire will consume the tents of bribery."*

You can see how scary and strongly-worded the passages of the Bible that refer to bribery are. When the Bible says that fire will consume the tent of bribery then it tells us that as many people who are engaging in bribery in any form are calling for fire and brimstones upon themselves. And when you say that fire will consume, it is not just the burning fire that is being referred to here but the consuming fire. There is a difference, a fire that consumes leaves nothing behind. It totally destroys without trace.

In view of this, will you still have the heart to take the next bribe? Can you prosper otherwise? Yes, you can. The Bible says that it is God who gives the power to our hands to make wealth in line with the covenant He has with Abraham. Are we partakers of that covenant? Yes! We came into the lineage of Abraham and became benefactors of his covenant through the blood of Jesus. But God does not work against Himself, so every time that we introduce a factor that is not of God in our situation, we take God out of it. We then want to do things in our own way, and by our own power. The Bible says *except the LORD builds the house, the labourers work in vain* (Psalm 127:1).

I want you to cast your mind back to recollect how many people you know who used to be rich, or who used to be powerful, or used to be in position of influence, but who have since disappeared and their story is a sorry one to hear today. That is the heritage of the man who built his wealth on unrighteousness. Unrighteous gain would destroy.

In Proverbs 10:25, the Bible says *"When the whirlwind passes by, the wicked is no more, but a righteous man has an everlasting foundation."*

It's so easy to build castles. But the castles you build from bribery will not survive the whirlwind when it comes. If you look around in some high-profile residential estates you will see many abandoned buildings. If you investigate the stories behind some of those abandoned buildings, you will find that the owners were making a lot of money from bribery because they were once occupying a particular office at some point in time, but when they were ousted out of office, the building stopped.

Don't build castles in the air, they will come tumbling down. Bribery is destructive. As you destroy some people in the course of collecting the bribe so do you destroy yourself and your generation after you as well.

Should you pay a bribe depending on some peculiar circumstance? There is no circumstance that justify paying a bribe. How can one separate a bribe from a gift? When what you give is not intended to influence or to make the other person work in your favour, then it is not a bribe. If you compete for a contract somewhere and you get it fairly, and somebody in position there helps you in the course of the work and gives you all the corporate support you need to be able to deliver, and in appreciation of the role that person played, not because he demanded for anything, or by pre-negotiation, but of your own free will, you choose to give him something, that is a gift or gratification, it is not a bribe. There is nothing wrong in appreciating people who are useful to you in the course of what you do. But if you pre-arrange it, it's a bribe, no matter what you say, even when you did not negotiate the amount.

Someone may ask, is it right to give a tip? If someone renders a service that you appreciate, you give him a tip. There is nothing wrong with that.

What about if you find yourself accosted by a policeman across the road? The truth is that we tend to position ourselves in a situation that allows people to ask us for a bribe. Firstly, because we haven't done the right thing; if you drive a vehicle

BRIBERY & CORRUPTION

on the road and you don't have a driver's license, vehicle insurance, or other necessary documents, you have left the room for someone to take advantage of you or extort from you.

If for example you are in business and you don't have enough information about your line of business. For instance, the government has banned shoes and bags and their accessories, but the government has not banned shoes for women. But many people who are in the shoes business have not even taken the time to get the correct information on what the government has said. And so you could arrive at the airport and some custom officer who wants to take advantage of what the government has said or not said will come to you and say that the good is contraband, and for you to bring it in you have to give him certain amount of money. And because you have not done your homework you begin to panic and want to negotiate with him. The Bible says 'my people perish for lack of knowledge' (Hosea 4:6).

The customs are supposed to value what you have brought and charge you the duties based on the rate that the government has stipulated. And then you go to the bank at the airport, pay the duty, bring the paper back, they sign and you leave. What will it cost you? It is time. You have a choice to do it or to pay the man that wants to extort from you.

We have many roles to play if we want this country to change for the better. We have to take the decisions if we do not want those in authority to continue to use their authority against us. Their salaries are paid from our taxes. It's a very large issue, while I seem to have flogged it in different directions I am honestly crying out and I am hoping that there are people who are willing to cry out with me for us to build a country that I, as a person, have always dreamt of, and one that I believe even you will like to be a citizen of.

Ours is a great country. There are many good things about Nigeria and Nigerians. We can fight this evil that is called bribery and we can win. It takes my commitment and yours to change our country for the better.

Other aspects of corruption, which affect our lives on a daily basis, are embezzlement, misappropriation of funds, diversion of funds; a lot of fancy names for an act that at the end of the day is merely a misuse of position or authority against the same people we are called to serve.

BRIBERY & CORRUPTION

I still have some biblical references to cite. It is interesting to note that God actually covers all issues that we as humans have to deal with on a daily basis. If we just take a little time and read our bible, and find out what His position is, we will not be quick to do so many things that we do and therefore bring troubles upon ourselves.

Let me read this interesting passage for you, it is in Jeremiah 17:11, *"As a partridge that broods but does not hatch, so is he who gets riches but not by right. It will leave him in the middle of his days and at the end he will be a fool."*

When someone is embezzling, misappropriating public funds, or stealing in short, he is like a partridge that is brooding but does not hatch, because the hatching part is the process of completion that God has ordained. And a man who is stealing can never be complete in his process, it's like a short-circuited wire, it rises fast and then fizzles out, that's exactly how it is. For a season he may appear like a superstar, and all of a sudden the light is sucked out of that star.

A man that embezzles from his office or from public funds is getting riches not by right. When someone steals salaries that should be paid to workers he is getting rich but not by right, when one steals the salaries of teachers or diverts it into an account for a season and pays them three months later, while they do not benefit from the interests generated by the money he puts in a fixed deposit, such person is getting riches but not by right. When someone steals goods that belong to his company, the state, or to someone else, and sells it off to enrich himself, he is getting rich but not by right.

For the wealth to leave in the middle of one's days is to leave him hanging with an incomplete system. He will realise that he has not really accomplished anything. The route he follows that he assumes is leading to a great glory will just disappear in his very eyes. Then he will amount to nothing, because ill-gotten wealth brings no peace or happiness.

Ezekiel 34:2-3 says, *"Woe to the shepherds of Israel who feed themselves, should not the shepherd feed the flock?"*

Do you know what "woe" is? It's a curse, destruction, disdain, anything evil, that is what woe represents. Something negative that you do not want to happen in your life, that is 'woe.' God is asking us a question in this passage. When you are a shepherd and have a flock of sheep, is it not your responsibility to feed them? Is it not your responsibility to use what has been committed into your hand for the good of those who are under your care? As a local government chairman, should the bad roads in your neighbourhood that are under your jurisdiction not be fixed when funds have been released, for the benefit of the people and the common good of all? Should the salaries of the teachers not be paid? As the MD of a company, should the salaries of your workers not be paid when the money is available?

That passage continues thus, *"You eat the fat and clothe yourselves with the wool; you slaughter the fatlings but you do not feed your flock"* (Ezekiel 34:3).

That means you have the best, the best of food, the best of garments, the best of houses, the beat of cars, the best of everything. But you do not do that which you are meant to do. You do not attend to the responsibility you have been assigned. The Bible says 'woe unto you.'

It is baffling to note how much disregard we have developed for the word of God. We act as if it is of no effect; we act as if they are just mere words

BUSINESS HIS WAY

without power. But history tells a different story. God is an awesome God; you do not want to be visited by His wrath. Yet He is a God of integrity, One that will keep His word, the Bible says 'heaven and earth may pass away, but not a word of God will pass without being fulfilled.'

My dear brothers and sisters, fellow Nigerians, let us fear God, and by so doing let us do what is right.

8

BUSINESS FAQs

QUESTION 1: *How does one convert his gift into business, or how can one start a business in a situation where he doesn't have a good financial backing?*

ANSWER: Converting your gift or talent into a business is a function of both your passion and your interest. If you have identified your gift and you are passionate enough in your desire to turn it into a commercial venture, you will begin to see things that other people around you do not see.

Sometimes, the idea that will come to you may not be what nobody else has done before. It may be a case of you seeing what you are interested in doing, but you can identify flaws in the way it is being done, and you know you can do it much better. The solution you have to the problem that currently exists is in itself an opportunity that you can take advantage of to set up a business.

The issue then is, having identified such a situation, how does it become a business, especially if you don't have money? The Bible says we should not despise the days of humble beginning. One of the biggest challenges of this generation is that many entrepreneurs, while trying to start a business, think that there is no other way to start except in a big way. Therefore, there are a lot of people with a business plan that has a large amount attached to it, but there is nobody to give them that kind of figure. And because they cannot get the target amount, the project never takes off. For every business idea you have, there is a small, start-up or "small beginning" version of it.

Let me use myself as an example: I read Chemistry at the university, although I had wanted

BUSINESS FAQs

to study Architecture, because I love designs and creating things. However, after my Youth Corps Service, I had an opportunity to work in a Furniture company.

I only wanted to work there for a short time before heading for the bank like most of my contemporaries who graduated in the '80s. But as it turned out, I lasted there shorter than I thought. While there, I realised that selling furniture and advising customers on how to use them was natural to me. But then I did not like the way my employers ran their business.

I saw many flaws in what they did. I saw a lack of integrity that I was passionate about enough to want to do differently by myself. And when I had an opportunity to start the business with someone, I jumped at it without even thinking twice, simply because it was something I wanted to do. It never occurred to me then that we could fail, or that we didn't even have enough money to start with, there were many things I didn't think about.

Now, I'm not saying you shouldn't think through your plans. Think through your plans as much as you can, but note that many things will not be defined at the beginning. One thing you can do is this - which is what I did then- in the furniture industry, every carpenter comes with his tools. So in essence, I did not need to buy tools for carpenters to work. All I needed to do was to get the carpenters that would work. So you may need to outsource some of the tasks in the process of your work to specialists who are more equipped to do them best.

Secondly, I could not afford the machines I needed to do major works on the wood. But they let out those machines at the saw mill, and there were machinists working there also. So I would tell them what I wanted to do, and how I wanted it done; since they have the machines and the machinists they would work out the processes for me as if I were the one who did it. I just paid for the services and I would take the components back to my carpenters to put them together.

In term of spraying our furniture, we also couldn't afford a compressor and a spraying gun at that time. But I found out that I could also rent both compressor and spraying gun on a daily basis. And those were the choices I made then. In fact, we started our work in an uncompleted building beside my chief carpenter's house, while some of the works were also done at the backyard of my father's house.

I want you to note that I was already a graduate at this time, and most of my mates were already pursuing a career in banks. So mine seemed like a very unattractive course to follow, but I was passionate enough for me to be willing to make the sacrifices required.

What you need to realize is that if the business line you want to operate is one you have a natural talent for plus a desire to transform to an enterprise, you will be willing to make the necessary sacrifices to see it materialize.

There were many things I learnt at the budding stage of my business which I wouldn't have learnt if I had a father who gave me a fully equipped factory with the full complimentary of some staff to work for me from day one. I probably would have failed, and the business would have collapsed. There are many mistakes you can only make when you are small, which you can't afford to make when you are big.

So, don't kill your dream because of finance or any other challenge you might encounter. Firstly, you owe yourself the responsibility of identifying that God has really called you to the business you want to do. If He has, He will provide what you need to succeed in it. If you seek Him prayerfully and you are committed to what you are doing; and you are willing to pay the price, with integrity and character, you can build an organization from the scratch to the very top.

QUESTION 2: *I am a very adventurous, young woman. I have always dreamt of running my own business some day. But my husband does not seem to be in support of my plans. He prefers me to stay in paid employment. I'm not happy with the way I am right now, what do you advise me to do?*

ANSWER: I will not advise you to defy your husband. Because if you don't have your husband's support, you are not likely to go far in whatever you plan to do. If you really want to pursue your dreams, you will have to find a way of getting it across to your husband. You have to show seriousness and convince him that it's something you really want to do, something you are good at.

The reason men don't like their wife to go into business is because a lot of women do not seem to

BUSINESS FAQs

know how to manage the independence that business brings. And when you succeed at this, it becomes another challenge to manage the success at the same time with managing your home. Most men are afraid that when a woman is empowered in business or a major career, she will become uncontrollable.

However, your husband too has a master. As the Bible says that you, as a wife, should submit to him, he himself owes submission to God. You can go on your knees and pray to God, if He truly wants you to pursue the venture then He will speak to your husband. And you can trust that God will help you.

I am a married woman and, at the same time, a businessperson. And I know that it is very easy when your husband is on your side in whatever venture you aspire to do. I'm blessed to have married a man who gave me the needed support that has made it possible for me to succeed in pursuing my own dreams. So, if you stay with it and you are sincere about what you want to do, and you are also walking according to the Word of God as a wife in your home, eventually your husband will give his blessing to your request.

Just don't try to prove a point, don't say 'it is my life and I'm going to do what I want with it'. It's not a case of saying "I will do it, whatever it takes" or suffering in silence. It's more about walking along the path that will help you to achieve balance.

You don't want a successful business without a successful home. It will only be one side of your life. God created you first as a woman, secondly as a wife, and then as a mother. The best kind of success you can have is to succeed in all three, and you can do it. You just need a lot of wisdom to balance it, and the only place you can get that is from God. The wisdom of the world tells you otherwise and many women are in trouble today on account of that. So, prayerfully seek to find the balance, and with wisdom you will eventually get there.

QUESTION 3: *I am currently in a paid employment, with a good salary and fringe benefits. However, I have discovered the gifts of God in me, which has nothing to do with what I am doing right now. I really want to do the will of God for my life, and do business with the talent that He has deposited in me. At the same time, I don't want to just walk out of the security of my present job.*

BUSINESS FAQs

Please advise me on what to do. Do I start my business now or wait until later?

ANSWER: Well, later is the convenient answer for most people. But the problem with waiting until later is that "later" never ends. There is always a later in your life and that may just be the day you go home to be with the Lord, without your ever accomplishing what you are called to do.

Many who have the security of a job find it very difficult to move out because of fear: fear of tomorrow, fear of where the salary is going to come from, fear of failure, among others. It is true that many people have left their job to do a business and have failed. But most times, they did not fail because they made that move but because they took some wrong decisions or followed some wrong processes along the line.

Most of the time people are not sure of what they want to do. They do not do the due diligence of identifying their strengths or going through all the processes that are necessary for setting up. They just want to jump into one business idea that someone brought their way and invest their pension money in it. And within a short while, they lose it all.

If you are certain that God has called you, or that you have talents/skills in the area you want to pursue, take the time to do your homework very well. Research everything that you need to know about the type of business you want to do. Seek all the necessary information, counsel, and all the help you can get. Take the time to invest in your dream. Most people are not willing to do what is necessary; they just jump into business without taking the time to sort out all that will secure their success in the business. What you don't do now will cost you dearly at the end of the day.

If you want to change career and go into business if you believe that God has called you to it and you have done your homework very well you have no reason whatsoever not to succeed. What you need is the boldness to step out and dare to do. The Bible says the children of God are as bold as a lion. The lion is not afraid of anything. Once you have God on your side, you should take that step.

In my own words, I would say jump. The worst that can happen is that you will fall. And if you fall, so what? You get up and continue. Those who are afraid of failure will never succeed. Every successful person I know has failed at one thing or the other on his way to success. The lessons you learn in failure are lessons that will help you to succeed.

QUESTION 4: *I am running a family business, which I inherited from my father, but I am not fulfilled or satisfied with it. Even though it is quite a successful business, it is not what I really want to do. But my family members are looking up to me for the continuity of the business, what do you suggest that I do?*

ANSWER: You only have one life to live. And inasmuch as you have responsibilities to your larger family, you also have responsibilities to yourself. When the chips are down, you are the one who is going to account to God for what He has called you to do. And if what He has called you to specifically is not the same with what you are doing now because you inherited your father's business, then you need to address some pertinent issues.

The business you inherited might be successful because it is your father's calling. He fulfilled his calling and was able to build a successful business. Perhaps he didn't finish the job by raising a successor for it, because his son may not necessarily be the successor for his business.

Why don't you find a professional manager to run the business? Find someone who is competent in that kind of business and let him run the business for the family. You can be on the management board or act as an overseer to the management team. But you have the responsibility to pursue your own dreams. And if what you want to do is entirely different from your present occupation, then go ahead and do it.

The truth is, any time we do not do what is natural to us; we will not have full satisfaction. I know a gentleman who studied agriculture at the university and was employed to work in a bank. He did well in the bank, but he eventually realized that was not what he really wanted to do, even though he was quite comfortable with a good salary and other fringe benefits that come with a banking job.

He knew there was a void somewhere in his life, because what he really wanted to do was to run a poultry business. Of course, if you compare the life of a banker and that of a fledgling poultry farmer, you will realize this man would have to sacrifice many things. But because it was what he really wanted to do, he was willing to pay the price. Eventually, he left the bank and went in pursuit of his dream. The last time I saw him, he said he was more fulfilled doing what he was doing now in his poultry. And though he has to discard his fancy suits and is now mostly dressed in jeans and T-shirts, he is now more at home with himself.

My question to you is, are you satisfied or happy when you think about your job or your business every morning? If you are not, then you can still take a turnaround and pursue that which you are more inclined to do. It is never too late.

You might say 'I've been doing what I am presently doing for the past 20 years, what am I going to do now?'

Well, it's only twenty years. Why lose the entire years of your life instead? Besides, those twenty years are not entirely lost. There are things you have learnt in your present occupation that you can apply as you pursue your new venture. What is really important is that, at the end of your day, you would be able to say 'I have done everything I sought to do'.

BUSINESS HIS WAY

I'm sure you've heard of *Kentucky Fried Chicken*. Do you know at what age he started the business that is now known all over the world? He was retired at age 65. He had no income except for his government benefits. It was out of the frustration of knowing that his pension and benefits from government were not enough to sustain him and his family that he sought to do something else to increase his income.

He realized that he was good at making chicken in a way that is peculiar to him alone. He tried it out commercially, and the rest is history. It turned out to be a major success. Now *Kentucky Fried Chicken* is seen in several cities all over the world. That was a man of 65. I'm sure you are not that old yet. So there is still so much you can do. Time is always available as long as you are alive.

I encourage you to seek after your dream. Pursue that which you know will give you joy. So that at the end of your days, you can look back and say, 'that which I always dreamt of doing, even though I didn't start off doing it early enough, I still had a chance to pursue it, and I'm glad I did'.

QUESTION 5: *I listened to you speak on partnership, but I want to know how I can practically apply these principles?*

ANSWER: Partnership is a very practical issue. Before venturing into it as a means of business, you need to take some practical approaches.

Firstly, if you decide to do a particular line of business and you find a partner you will like to work with, it is important that you go through every process of identifying all the details. Set a time aside for yourself; write out both your short-term and long-term vision for the business. Write out all your expectations as well as all other issues to be covered in the partnership; the way you want the relationship to be between you and your partner, write them all out on your own independent of your partner.

Then tell your partner to do the same. Let him make a list of all the issues that are important to him: the things he would like to incorporate into the business, the basis of your relationship, etc. Then take time to run through every item that is listed in each person's blueprint one at a time. When you finish with that, you will discover that you have some things in common; if this is not the case, then you two have no basis for the partnership in the first place.

As a result of this exercise, you will find out that there are things your partner desires that are not important to you, and that there are things you desire that are not important to your partner. Discuss all of these and don't consider any of them as unimportant. For every point of disagreement on both sides, come to an agreement that is acceptable to both of you. Write it in your memorandum of agreement; get an arbitrator to witness it, and that becomes the document that will form the basis of your partnership.

Having defined a lot of things at the beginning, you will find out that it's a lot easier to run together. Don't be embarrassed about anything, don't try to impress your partner, ask the most stupid questions. It is always easier to deal with all issues at the beginning. Consider all the parties that may be involved around you and the kind of influence they may have on your relationship. Think about every imaginable thing, and at the end of the day come to an agreement.

QUESTION 6: *Are there any spiritual implications for pulling out of a Partnership?*

ANSWER: I usually compare business partnership to a marital partnership. There are spiritual implications for pulling out of a marriage, because the Bible does not encourage divorce. However, in your terms of agreement in partnership, you can decide in advance the situation that may necessitate one party pulling out of the partnership. There is no spiritual implication to it.

The Bible says you should not be unequally yoked, which means that the only requirement for going into a partnership is to ensure that both of you are of like faith. That way your considerations will be similar. That is why the Bible talks about unequal yoke. It's talking about spiritual yoking. But if you then decide to separate from a partnership, as long as you have fulfilled all the legal issues and you are at peace with one another you can pull out of the partnership.

Question 7: *My financial partner, who has a 60% shares in our venture, always insists on having his way* in major issues that affect the operations of the company. Though I am the operating manager because of my technical skills, my partner, who is a domineering man, always interferes in the affairs of the company. He wants us to employ his candidates and do some other things his own way. Do you advise me to pull out of this partnership, or do I stay put and begin to exercise my authority a bit more?

ANSWER: This is one of the problems you face when you did not detail the terms of your relationship at the beginning. What you need at this point is not to quit but to have an open conversation with your partner. It seems to me that you have never even voiced out your feelings to him yet. Sit him down and make him realize your contributions and value to the company. Even though he is the majority shareholder; which gives him majority power, but because you are the technical partner, you are also empowered. And the operator in most cases can even be more powerful than the financial partner because he controls the day-to-day activities of the business.

So you have to recognize your authority in terms of the responsibility you hold and exercise it.

Tell him the likely consequence of his undue interference in your day-to-day activities, and the detrimental effects of hiring unqualified family members to work in the company.

Don't be quick to jump out of what you worked for, sit and discuss things together. If, after discussing these with him, you are not able to agree on a solution, then you can start discussing pulling out. You may try to buy him out of the company. But seek peace first, and if that fails, you can then consider the alternative.

QUESTION 8: *My partner and I are both Christians. We have been in partnership now for eight years when we were both singles. Now we are married and my partner is talking of bringing his wife, who is a qualified accountant, into the firm. I am not so disposed to this move because I fear they might play a fast one on me in the long run. Please advise me on what to do, should I say 'yes' and allow my partner's wife into the company, or should I put my feet down and refuse?*

ANSWER: How you feel about the issue is already obvious. You are not comfortable with the idea of your partner's wife coming into the business. And I quite understand your position because such arrangement can create problems in most cases. Not because they want to cheat on you, but because the question of who she would listen to? If there is a case where she needs to be neutral, to whom will her allegiance be between you and her husband? Operationally there would be a problem.

What about you, do you want to bring your own wife into the company as well? I can only see confusion in that set-up. If the women don't step on each other's toes, they will cause the men to do so. That is not to say we women are perpetual troublemakers, but in an environment of business, you need to do without emotion. But once you start bringing in your wives, emotions will be set in and rationality will fly away.

So, it is better for you to be honest with your partner about your feelings. I don't know what your terms stated, but if you have considered all relevant issues at the beginning, you would have dealt with how to deal with spouses and relatives in the business.

QUESTION 9: *How do I determine who to enter into partnership with?*

ANSWER: The first requirement biblically is that you must be of like faith. But that, in itself, is not a license for you to be careless in forming alliances. The fact that someone professes to be a Christian, or goes to the same church with you, does not make him a good candidate for partnership.

Two brothers are so different even though they are of the same blood. Even twins are not entirely the same, so why would you want to go into business with someone without checking out details about him: do you have similar character? Do you desire the same thing? Do you have natural inclinations that can work together? Are your views and long-term aspirations the same?

I am sure you won't just marry anybody because she is a Christian. The same principle applies when it comes to partnership; you need to thoroughly check out the person you want to partner with.

QUESTION 10: *A born again friend of mine and I are going into a partnership. We are both technologists, and are not so versed in the area of business. What are the issues we should resolve and how do we go about making our venture a success?*

ANSWER: I believe some of the things I have mentioned above would have answered your question. Just make sure you do the due diligence and be thorough about it.

You should both ask yourselves, what are the strengths you both are bringing to the table? What are the shortcomings you have, and how can you make up for each other? Like you said, you are both technocrats, maybe you don't have an accounting knowledge or business management skills, find the people who have these skills, employ them and pay them well so that they can have a sense of commitment to the business. And whatever is necessary to bring the business to the height you dream for it, give it to it. But make sure that you are very clear about what you want to do.

If you are both technically competent, who is going to be the boss? Will it be both of you? Somebody must always have the last say; somebody must be in charge of one thing or the other. Agree as to how you will run the organization. Who is going to be in charge of management? Who is going to be in charge of design? Separate the responsibilities with clarity and don't say 'we are both the chief executives'. You

can't have two chief executives; it's not going to work. Titles are not important; it is getting the business done that is.

Another thing you need to do is to acknowledge each other's strengths and weaknesses. One of you might be stronger in dealing with people and interacting with customers than the other. This person who is more inclined to dealing with and managing people can handle the management aspect of the business, while the other person takes charge of the operations. This doesn't change the fact that you both hold equal shares in the company and, at the end of the day, the profits will be shared according to your shareholding.

But you need to use the assets of each other for the benefit of the company. It's not about what kind of role, but what value you bring to the table. It takes a lot of openness, maturity and respect for each other's ideals to "click" in partnership. You cannot afford to be envious of each other, which is why it is important that you have everything clearly defined so that you don't start to fret when someone from outside call you a fool for whatever reason. There is a lot of external interference, which underscores the need for you to be matured about partnership if you decide to go into it.

You cannot afford to say the other person is the only one getting all the benefits, if such are natural benefits that come with the kind of assignment he does for the company. You have to learn to accept that he is doing what he does for both of you, because at the end of the day, the proceeds of that work will come back to both of you. Moreover, if he were to be an independent employee that his assignment requires those facilities, would you have had any grudge against it? You need to have an open mind where partnership is concerned. And make sure you define the roles.

QUESTION 11: *I am the only believer on the board of my family business. The Bible says we should "not be unequally yoked together with unbelievers", should I pull out of this business or should I continue with them?*

ANSWER: Well, it depends on what kind of family business you are talking about. If you are in a business with your father or your mother, remember the Bible also says we should honour

our parents. That is one commandment in the Bible that comes with a promise and it is, in itself, a principle you should obey.

Work with your father. Respect and honour him without necessarily compromising or sinning. A problem can only arise if you think that by remaining in that business, you would have to walk against the commands of God. But also note that God might have placed you in that business so that you can influence it positively with the principles you have imbibed as a Christian.

The fact that you are now a Christian is not enough reason to jump out of the business. I think you will be able to do more good through your interactions with them than merely instigating resentment for your faith through your actions. Most Christians are usually immature in the way they handle this kind of situation, especially young believers who just accepted Christ. To them everything else usually becomes totally negative in the light of their new found truth.

There is usually love in a family. And you can make them understand the basics of what you are learning from your new faith and how you want to apply them in the family business. With a lot of love and understanding, you are likely to reach them with your message.

QUESTION 12: *I listen to your teachings on partnership and I enjoy it a lot. My question is, does partnership have an age limit? As a young man of 28, can I go into business with someone my father's age?*

ANSWER: Partnership has no age limit. But you need to consider certain issues, if you at 28 want to go into partnership with someone between 58 and 60 years of age, would you see things the same way? Would the age gap between you not be so pronounced as to create some crises?

On the other hand, this could be beneficial because there is a lot of wisdom that comes with age that your older partner can avail you with. You just need to consider the issues involved; age limit is really no barrier but how the two of you fit together in partnership, and what the terms of your partnership states.

Will you be bold enough to disagree when you need to? You know we are all brought up to revere age. How are you going to strike the balance between respecting an elderly person and expressing your opinion as a partner in business? These are some of the issues that you might have to deal with. Once you can deal with such realities, then there is nothing wrong with going into partnership with an older person.

QUESTION 13: *I am a very ambitious young man with lofty dreams and visions of the great things I want to achieve in life, both in business and ministry. However, I'm presently engaged to a lady who is very brilliant. But apart from that she has no drive or motivation to "conquer territories". My fiancé appears satisfied with the basic things of life. Now her lack of self-motivation is a source of concern to me, as I do not feel challenged by her. And any attempt on my part to challenge her to do things is met with resentment. Please tell me what to do, should I break the courtship and look for someone who is more like-minded to marry? Please reply fast!*

ANSWER: I think there are many issues here. If a woman doesn't challenge you, that is something you have to learn how to deal with, because the bible says two cannot walk together except they agree (Amos 3:3). If you feel that she is not going to motivate you and you want a different kind of person, which is what you seem to want from the tone of your mail, then obviously, this marriage might not work. Not because there is anything wrong with the woman because that's the way she is.

You have said she is a brilliant person, only that she is just satisfied with the little things of life. It's not having the big things or the little things that matters. It is about you finding what works for you and what gives you peace.

Now for another man, a woman like this is just what he needs because she would be a balancing factor in his life. And if that's what he wants, that's what will work for him. But if what you want is a woman who is more like you, who will motivate and challenge you, then that is what I will advise you to go for.

If you are trying to change your fianceé, you are going to run into trouble because you do not have the capacity to change another person. God has made us all in different forms. The only thing we can do quite successfully is to change ourselves, and then hope that by changing ourselves we can affect the people around us.

My question to you is "are you willing to change to suit what she wants as well? Maybe she really doesn't want a man that will change her into what she is not. And if she tries to be who you want her to be she will probably fail at it eventually and she will live a miserable life. You might be happy with what she tries to become for your sake, but what about her? It's got to be a symbiotic relationship. It must be a win-win situation and not a win-lose. She shouldn't lose so that you can have what you want. You've got to be what she wants and she's got to be what you want, and both of you must be able to help each other to fulfil your dreams and your ambitions without losing yourself.

QUESTION 14: *What do you consider as ideal entrepreneurship?*

ANSWER: Ideal entrepreneurship is hard to define. Entrepreneurship is about birthing your dream and bringing to reality in economic or creative terms a dream in your heart, something you have imagined and are able to turn into a business or a source of changing life, or a source of producing something. That is what entrepreneurship is about.

For different people, depending on their personality and kind of character or the environment where they operate, it can be different things. An entrepreneur in Nigeria deals with different issues compared to the entrepreneur in the United States or the one in China. We have different challenges, the insurmountable situations we have to cope with to survive in an environment as ours probably does not exist for the entrepreneur that needs to set up a business in the States or in Europe. The environments are totally different and your ability to overcome whatever those challenges are, no matter which environment you are, is probably what will make your entrepreneurship ideal for your situation. So it's different, it's even different from Lagos to Kano, Port-Harcourt or Ibadan, it is different scenarios. You have to find what is ideal for your own environment. But the thing that is a common factor to all entrepreneurs is that you started up thinking about something and you put everything together or overcame every situation in order to bring it to reality. That is an entrepreneur and what makes it ideal varies from location to location.

Printed in the United States
143795LV00001BA/61/P